S0-DFI-018

Hymns III

Church Hymnal Series III

The Church Hymnal Corporation
800 Second Avenue, New York, N.Y. 10017

Copyright © 1979 by The Church Pension Fund

All rights reserved. No part of this book may be reproduced, stored in a retrieval system, or transmitted, in any form or by any means, electronic, mechanical, photocopying, recording, or otherwise, without the written permission of The Church Pension Fund.

Every effort has been made to trace the owner or holder of each copyright. If any rights have been inadvertently infringed upon, the Publishers ask that the omission be excused and agree to make the necessary corrections in subsequent editions.

The Church Pension Fund
800 Second Avenue
New York, N.Y. 10017

ISBN: 0-89869-012-9 (spiral)
013-7 (soft)

Preface

The Hymnal, to be responsive to the worship life of the Church it seeks to serve, must constantly undergo a process of enrichment. The history of the Hymnal of the Episcopal Church reflects this responsiveness through its many editions that have appeared since the year 1789 when the General Convention of the Church included metrical psalms and a small number of hymns in the first Prayer Book of the Church. *Hymns III*, the most recent effort in this ongoing process, has been created in direct response to the expanded liturgical and musical opportunities afforded in the new Prayer Book.

Recognizing the needs created by a three-year lectionary and the enriched liturgical possibilities of the new Prayer Book, *Hymns III* expands certain sections of the present official Hymnal of the Episcopal Church. This book reflects the study of a large number of hymnals in current use throughout the Christian Church. In areas where literary materials were found inadequate, new translations were commissioned. To assure consistency with the thought and language of the new Prayer Book and the theology of the Church, a Theological Committee under the guidance of Dr. Charles Price of Virginia Theological Seminary reviewed all texts.

Musically, the book is enhanced by the inclusion of a number of new tunes not presently found in the Hymnal. Several are experimental in nature, using new sounds and styles. Opportunities are afforded for the use of instruments other than the organ or piano and a large number of descants and fauxbourdon are included.

In response to the need of congregations who find the use of chant difficult, *Hymns III* contains canticles of the new Book of Common Prayer in meter. Several are in new translation while others come from the rich repository of the Church's treasury of literature.

In the preparation of this book, the Hymn Committee of the Standing Commission on Church Music under the chairmanship of Raymond F. Glover of St. Paul's Church, Richmond, Virginia, has sought the advice and help of hymnologists and musicians throughout the Church. Special appreciation is extended to Dr. Marion Hatchett of the School of Theology of the University of the South for his extensive work in the initial planning of this collection and to Miss Deborah Wallace for her editorial work. *Hymns III* is presented in the spirit of past committees who sought to provide the Church with a hymnody responsive to its needs, reflective of its great literary and musical heritage and sensitive to the creativity of contemporary authors and composers.

Performance Notes

Hymns III, by its very nature, serves a twofold function; one, liturgical, the other, musical.

The enriched liturgical life of the Church today has created expanded musical needs. The table of contents reveals the broad liturgical scope of this collection with many additional hymns for such times as Advent, the Baptism of our Lord, Easter and Pentecost. In addition, the book suggests the use of certain portions of hymns on specific Sundays during the liturgical season. Also, many metrical versions of canticles and psalms are included as alternatives for chant settings.

On the musical side, the collection is practical as well as inventive with new sonorities and varied performance potential. Many settings have three-part textures while others have very practical accompaniments which will sound good in any liturgical setting. For example, where appropriate, guitar chords are provided and special directions have been included for the use of the guitar with or without a keyboard instrument. Special note should be made of the use of the capo when the key of the keyboard version is not ideally suited to guitar. Also, for the setting of the Spiritual, "Go Tell it on the Mountain," the compilers chose an indigenous harmonization best suited for performance on the piano. In several cases, the use of strings and/or wind instruments is suggested. All these recommendations are intended as a springboard for the creative person who seeks constantly growing, imaginative performances of hymnody.

Last of all, please note the inclusion of metronome marks as indication of tempi to avoid the frequent confusion and vagueness prevalent in the past. These metronome indications, when possible, have been chosen to fit the larger rhythmic pulse of the music, thus enhancing the realization of the musical line. Further, for successful performance, several settings in *Hymns III* require the faithful use of these tempo marks. However, in almost every case, these indications must be adapted to the acoustical conditions of the spaces in which hymns are used, the size of the congregation, and the occasion when they are performed.

We hope that the use of *Hymns III* with these guidelines will lead to more vital hymn singing by our congregations.

— The Standing Commission on Church Music

Table of Contents
with Cross References

H-112	Go tell it on the mountain
H-113a	On this day, earth shall ring
H-113b	On this day, earth shall ring
H-114	Today our God, of his great mercy

Also the following:

H-190	All glory be to God on high (*Gloria in excelsis*)
H-203	Glorious the day when Christ was born
H-246	Where is this stupendous stranger

New Year

| H-115 | Great God, we sing that mighty hand |

Epiphany

| H-116 | When Christ's appearing was made known |
| H-117 | When Christ's appearing was made known |

For the First Sunday after The Epiphany: The Baptism of our Lord

H-118a	The sinless one to Jordan came
H-118b	The sinless one to Jordan came
H-119	When Jesus went to Jordan's stream
H-120	Christ, when for us you were baptized

Also the following:

| H-116 | When Christ's appearing was made known |

For the Last Sunday after the Epiphany:

| H-121 | Christ upon the mountain peak |
| H-122 | Christ upon the mountain peak |

Lent

H-123	Wilt thou forgive that sin
H-124a	Wilt thou forgive that sin
H-124b	Wilt thou forgive that sin
H-125	Lift high the cross

Also the following:

H-217	My song is love unknown
H-219	Nature with open volume stands
H-227	Out of the depths I cry to thee (*Psalm 130*)

H-245a	What wondrous love is this, O my soul
H-245b	What wondrous love is this, O my soul

For Maundy Thursday:

H-202	God is love, and where true love is *(Ubi caritas)*
H-213	Jesu, Jesu, fill us with your love
H-247a	Where charity and love prevail *(Ubi caritas)*
H-247b	Where charity and love prevail *(Ubi caritas)*
H-248	Where true love and charity are found *(Ubi caritas)*

For the Great Vigil of Easter:

H-232	Sing now with joy *(Song of Miriam)*
H-126,-139	

Easter

H-126	Christ Jesus lay in death's strong bands
H-127	Christ is arisen
H-128	Christ the Lord is risen again
H-129	Christ the Lord is risen again
H-130	Christians, haste your vows to pay
H-131	Come away to the skies
H-132	Good Christians all, rejoice and sing
H-133	I know that my Redeemer lives
H-134a	Now the green blade riseth
H-134b	Now the green blade riseth
H-135	On earth has dawned this day of days
H-136	The Lamb's high banquet called to share
H-137	The Lamb's high banquet called to share
H-138	Through the Red Sea brought at last
H-139	This joyful Eastertide

Also the following:

H-203	Glorious the day when Christ was born
H-224	O love of God, how strong and true
H-225	O love of God, how strong and true
H-234	Sing, ye faithful, sing with gladness
H-236	The gates of death are broken through

Ascension

H-140	A hymn of glory let us sing

H-141	A hymn of glory let us sing
H-142	Christ, above all glory seated
H-143	O Lord most high, eternal King
H-144	O Lord most high, eternal King

Also the following:

H-230	Rejoice, the Lord is King
H-234	Sing, ye faithful, sing with gladness

Pentecost

H-145	To thee, O Comforter divine
H-146a	Come down, O Spirit, Love Divine *(Veni Creator Spiritus)*
H-146b	Come down, O Spirit, Love Divine *(Veni Creator Spiritus)*
H-147	Come, Holy Ghost, God and Lord
H-148	Hail this joyful day's return
H-149	Hail this joyful day's return
H-150	Holy Spirit, font of light *(Veni Sancte Spiritus)*
H-151	Holy Spirit, font of light *(Veni Sancte Spiritus)*
H-152	Upon that Whitsun morning
H-153	O Holy Spirit, by whose breath *(Veni Creator Spiritus)*
H-154	O Holy Spirit, by whose breath *(Veni Creator Spiritus)*

Also the following:

H-167	O Holy Spirit, enter in
H-207a	Holy Ghost, dispel our sadness
H-207b	Holy Ghost, dispel our sadness
H-208	Holy Spirit, ever living
H-223a	O Holy Spirit, Lord of grace
H-223b	O Holy Spirit, Lord of grace
H-226	O Spirit of Life, O Spirit of God

For the First Sunday after Pentecost (Trinity Sunday):

H-169	Sing praise to our creator
H-190	All glory be to God on high *(Gloria in excelsis)*
H-210	How wondrous great, how glorious bright
H-222	O God, we praise thee, and confess *(Te Deum laudamus)*

For the Last Sunday after Pentecost:

H-142	Christ, above all glory seated
H-230	Rejoice, the Lord is King

Saints' Days and Holy Days

For the Presentation (February 2):

H-215   Lord, let your servant *(Nunc dimittis)*

The Annunciation (March 25):

H-155   The angel Gabriel
H-156a   The Christ whom earth and sea
H-156b   The Christ whom earth and sea
H-157   The Christ whom earth and sea

Also the following:

H-235   Tell out, my soul *(Magnificat)*

For the Visitation (May 31):

H-156a   The Christ whom earth and sea
H-156b   The Christ whom earth and sea
H-157   The Christ whom earth and sea
H-235   Tell out, my soul *(Magnificat)*

For the Nativity of Saint John the Baptist (June 24):

H-193   Blest be the God of Israel *(Benedictus Dominus Deus)*

For the Transfiguration (August 6):

H-121   Christ upon the mountain peak
H-122   Christ upon the mountain peak

For Saint Mary the Virgin (August 15):

H-156a   The Christ whom earth and sea
H-156b   The Christ whom earth and sea
H-157   The Christ whom earth and sea
H-235   Tell out, my soul *(Magnificat)*

For Holy Cross Day (September 14):

H-125   Lift high the cross

For Saint Michael and All Angels (September 29):

H-228   Praise the Lord! ye heavens adore him *(Psalm 148)*
H-249   Ye servants of God, your Master proclaim
H-250   Ye servants of God, your Master proclaim

For All Saints' Day (November 1):

H-176	For the bread which thou hast broken
H-194	Blessed are the poor in spirit

Evangelists

H-158	Come, pure hearts, in sweetest measure

Martyrs

H-159	King of the martyrs' noble band
H-160	King of the martyrs' noble band

For Thanksgiving and National Days:

H-189a	As those of old their first fruits brought
H-189b	As those of old their first fruits brought
H-204	God of mercy, God of grace (*Psalm 67*)

Morning

H-161	Morning has broken

Evening

H-162	O gracious Light, Lord Jesus Christ *(Phos hilaron)*
H-163	O gracious Light, Lord Jesus Christ *(Phos hilaron)*

Holy Baptism

H-164	All who believe and are baptized
H-165	Spirit of God, unleashed on earth
H-166a	Descend, O Spirit, purging flame
H-166b	Descend, O Spirit, purging flame
H-167	O Holy Spirit, enter in
H-168	Praise and thanksgiving be to our creator
H-169	Sing praise to our creator
H-170	We know that Christ is raised and dies no more
H-171	This is the Spirit's entry now

Also the following:

H-131	Come away to the skies

Another hymn suitable for use at the baptism of a child:

H-172	We praise you, Lord, for Jesus Christ

Holy Eucharist

H-173	Come, risen Lord, and deign to be our guest
H-174	Father, we thank thee who hast planted
H-177	Lord, enthroned in heavenly splendor
H-178	I come with joy to meet my Lord

Other hymns suitable for use immediately before or after the postcommunion prayer:

H-175	Completed, Lord, the Holy Mysteries
H-176	For the bread which thou hast broken

The following hymns are also suitable for use as a sequence:

H-214	Lord, be thy word my rule
H-229	Praise we now the word of grace

Marriage

H-179	Dear Father, in thy house today
H-180	O thou whose favor hallows all occasions

Another hymn suitable for use at the renewal of marriage promises:

H-181	O Father blest, we ask of you

For Ember Days and Ordination:

H-146a	Come down, O Spirit, Love Divine *(Veni Creator Spiritus)*
H-146b	Come down, O Spirit, Love Divine *(Veni Creator Spiritus)*
H-150	Holy Spirit, font of light *(Veni Sancte Spiritus)*
H-151	Holy Spirit, font of light *(Veni Sancte Spiritus)*
H-208	Holy Spirit, ever living
H-153	O Holy Spirit, by whose breath *(Veni Creator Spiritus)*
H-154	O Holy Spirit, by whose breath *(Veni Creator Spiritus)*
H-249	Ye servants of God, your Master proclaim
H-250	Ye servants of God, your Master proclaim

Burial

H-182	May choirs of angels lead you *(In paradisum)*
H-183	Give rest, O Christ *(Contakion)*
H-184	Into Paradise may the angels lead you *(In paradisum)*
H-185	May angels lead you into Paradise *(In paradisum)*
H-186	May angels lead you into Paradise *(In paradisum)*

Also the following:

H-133	I know that my Redeemer lives
H-212a	I to the hills (*Psalm 121*)
H-212b	I to the hills (*Psalm 121*)
H-216	Lord, thou hast searched me and dost know (*Psalm 139*)
H-218a	My shepherd will supply my need (*Psalm 23*)
H-218b	My shepherd will supply my need (*Psalm 23*)
H-237	The Lord's my shepherd, I'll not want (*Psalm 23*)

For the Consecration of a Church:

H-209a	How lovely are thy dwellings fair (*Psalm 84*)
H-209b	How lovely are thy dwellings fair (*Psalm 84*)

General Hymns

H-187	All creatures of our God and King
H-188	All my hope on God is founded
H-189a	As those of old their first fruits brought
H-189b	As those of old their first fruits brought
H-190	All glory be to God on high (*Gloria in excelsis*)
H-191	Be thou my vision
H-192	Blessèd Jesus, at thy word
H-193	Blest be the God of Israel (*Benedictus Dominus Deus*)
H-194	Blessèd are the poor in spirit (*Beatitudes*)
H-195	Come, let us join our cheerful songs (*Dignus es*)
H-196	Come, my Way, my Truth, my Life
H-197	Come, sound his praise abroad (*Psalm 95: Venite*)
H-198	Come, thou font of every blessing
H-199	Earth and all stars
H-200	Eternal Ruler of the ceaseless round
H-201a	Forgive our sins as we forgive
H-201b	Forgive our sins as we forgive
H-202	God is love, and where true love is (*Ubi caritas*)
H-203	Glorious the day when Christ was born
H-204	God of mercy, God of grace (*Psalm 67*)
H-205	Guide me, O thou great Jehovah
H-206	Help us to help each other, Lord
H-207a	Holy Ghost, dispel our sadness
H-207b	Holy Ghost, dispel our sadness
H-208	Holy Spirit, ever living

H-101

1 On this day, the first of days, God the Fa-ther's
2 On this day thee e-ter-nal Son o-ver death his
3 Fa-ther, who didst fash-ion me dead and bur-ied
4 Ho-ly Je-sus, may I be shine, sweet Spir-it,
5 Thou, who dost all gifts im-part, dwell with-in my
6 God, the bless-ed Three in One,

1 Name we praise, who, cre-a-tion's Lord and spring,
2 tri-umph won; on this day the Spir-it came
3 self to be, fill me with thy love di-vine,
4 here with thee; and, by love in-flamed, a-rise
5 in my heart; best of gifts thy-self be-stow;
6 heart a-lone; thou dost give thy-self to me:

1 did the world from dark-ness bring.
2 with his gifts of liv-ing flame.
3 let my ev-ery thought be thine.
4 un-to thee a sac-ri-fice.
5 make me burn thy love to know.
6 may I give my-self to thee. A-men.

Stanzas 1 and 2 would be appropriate as a sequence hymn during the Easter season.

text: *Die parente temporum* anonymous Latin hymn from the *Carcassone Breviary* (1745), translated by Henry W. Baker, 1861.

tune: *Gott sei Dank* [Lübeck], Johann A. Freylinghausen, 1704.

77.77

♩ = 104

Sunday

H-102

1 This is the day the Lord hath made, he
2 To - day he rose and left the dead, and
3 Ho - san - na to the a - noint - ed King, to
4 Blest . 'be the Lord, who comes to us with
5 Ho - san - na in the high - est strains the

1 calls the hours his own; let heaven re - joice, let
2 Sa - tan's em - pire fell; to - day the saints his
3 Da - vid's ho - ly Son! Help us, O Lord; de -
4 mes - sag - es of grace! Who comes, in God his
5 church on earth can raise; the high - est heavens in

1 earth be glad, and praise sur - round the throne.
2 tri - umphs spread, and all his won - ders tell.
3 scend and bring sal - va - tion from thy throne.
4 Fa - ther's name, to save our sin - ful race.
5 which he reigns shall give him no - bler praise.

Stanzas 1 and 2 would be appropriate as a sequence hymn during the Easter season.
text: Isaac Watts, 1719, *alt.*
tune: *Warwick*, Samuel Stanley, 1802.
Alternate tune, *Bristol*, The Hymnal, No. 7

8 6.8 6
♩ = 69

Sunday

H-103

1 Com - fort, com - fort ye my peo - ple, speak ye peace, thus saith our God;
2 Hark, the voice of one that cri - eth in the de - sert far and near,
3 Make ye straight what long was crook - ed, make the rough-er pla - ces plain;

com-fort those who sit in dark - ness mourn-ing 'neath their sor - rows' load.
call - ing us to new re - pent - ance since the king-dom now is here.
let your hearts be true and hum - ble, as be - fits his ho - ly reign.

Speak ye to Je - ru - sa - lem of the peace that waits for them;
Oh, that warn - ing cry o - bey! Now pre-pare for God a way;
For the glo - ry of the Lord now o'er earth is shed a - broad;

tell her that her sins I cov - er, and her war - fare now is o - ver.
let the val - leys rise to meet him and the hills bow down to greet him.
and all flesh shall see the to - ken that his word is nev - er bro - ken.

text: *Tröstet, tröstet meine Lieben*, Johann G. Olearius, 1671, translated
      by Catherine Winkworth, 1864, *alt.*　　　　　　　　　87.87.77.88

tune: *Psalm 42* [Bourgeois], Louis Bourgeois, 1551.　　　　♩. = 50

Advent

H-104

each verse louder

1 Je-sus came-the heavens a - dor - ing - came with peace from realms on high;
2 Je-sus comes a - gain in mer - cy, when our hearts are bowed with care:
3 Je-sus comes to hearts re - joic-ing, bring-ing news of sins for-given;
4 Je-sus comes on clouds tri-umph-ant, when the heavens shall pass a - way;

Je - sus came for our re - demp-tion, low - ly came on earth to die:
Je - sus comes a - gain in an - swer to our earn - est heart-felt prayer;
Je - sus comes in sounds of glad-ness, lead-ing souls re - deemed to heaven;
Je - sus comes a - gain in glo - ry; let us then our hom-age pay;

Al - le - lu - ia! Al - le - lu - ia! came in deep hu - mil - i - ty.
Al - le - lu - ia! Al - le - lu - ia! comes to save us from des - pair.
Al - le - lu - ia! Al - le - lu - ia! now the gate of death is riven.
Al - le - lu - ia! Al - le - lu - ia! till the dawn of end - less day

text: Godfrey Thring, 1862, *alt.*

tune: *Lowry*, Gerald Near, 1977. Music copyright, 1978 by The Church Pension Fund. All Rights Reserved.

87.87.87

♩ = 54

Advent

H-105

1 Lift up your heads, ye might-y gates; be-hold the King of glo-ry
2 Fling wide the por-tals of your heart; make it a tem-ple, set a-
3 Re-deem-er, come! we o-pen wide our hearts to thee; here, Lord, a-

waits. The King of kings is draw-ing near; the Sav-ior of the world is
part from earth-ly use for heaven's em-ploy, a-dorned with praise and love and
bide. Let us thy in-ner pres-ence feel, thy grace and love in us re-

here. For us sal-va-tion he doth bring, so let us all re-joice and
joy. So let your Sov-ereign en-ter in, and new and no-bler life be-
veal; thy Ho-ly Spir-it guide us on un-til our glo-rious goal is

sing: we praise thee, Fa-ther, now; Cre-a-tor, wise art thou!
gin: to thee, O God, be praise for word and deed and grace!
won. E-ter-nal praise and fame we of-fer to thy name! A-men.

This is a metrical version of Psalm 24.

text: *Macht hoch die Tür*, Georg Weissel, 1642, translated by Catherine
Winkworth, 1855, alt.   88.88.88.66

tune: *Macht hoch die Tür*, Johann A. Freylinghausen, 1704. From *The Lutheran
Hymnal*, © 1941 by Concordia Publishing House. Used by permission.   ♩. = 48

Advent

H-106

1 O Sav - ior, o - pen heav - en wide; and once a -
2 Then praise and hom - age we will bring to you, our

gain, this Ad - vent - tide, un - bar the por - tals,
Sav - ior, God, and King; and we will bless you,

Lord, we pray, that shut our hearts from you to - day.
and a - dore for ev - er and for ev - er more. A - men.

text: *O Heiland, reiss die Himmel auf,* Friedrich von Spee, 1623, translated
by John Rodgers. From *The Catholic Hymnal,* used by permission of
Benziger, a division of Glencoe Publishing Co., Inc.

88.88

tune: *O Heiland, reiss,* traditional German melody from Corner's *Gross
Catolisch Gesangbuch* (1625), harmonized by Frank Campbell-Watson.
From *The Catholic Hymnal,* used by permission of Benziger,
a division of Glencoe Publishing Co., Inc.

♩ = 112

Advent

H-107

1 Once he came in bless - ing, all our ills re - dress - ing;
2 Still he comes with - in us, still his voice would win us
3 Thus, if thou canst name him, not a - shamed to claim him,
4 One who thus en - dur - eth bright re - ward se - cur - eth.

came in like - ness low - ly, Son of God most ho - ly;
from the sins that hurt us; would to Truth con - vert us
but wilt trust him bold - ly nor dost love him cold - ly,
Come, then, O Lord Je - sus, from our sins re - lease us;

bore the cross to save us, hope and free-dom gave us.
from our fool-ish er - rors, ere he comes in ter - rors.
he will then re - ceive thee, heal thee, and for - give thee.
let us here con - fess thee till in heav'n we bless thee. A - men.

text: *Gottes Sohn ist kommen*, Johann Roh, 1544, translated by Catherine
Winkworth, 1853, *alt.*   66.66.66

tune: *Gottes Sohn ist kommen*, melody by Michael Weisse, harmonized by
Russell Schulz-Widmar, 1978. Harmony, copyright 1978 by The Church
Pension Fund. All Rights Reserved.   ♩ = 63

Advent

H-108

1 Pre - pare the way, O Zi - on! ye fear - ful deeps, rise high;
2 O Zi - on, he ap - proach - es, your Lord and King for ay;
3 Fling wide your por - tals, Zi - on, and hail your glo - rious King;
4 The throne which he as - cend - ed is fixed in heaven a - bove;

sink low, ye loft - y moun - tains, the Lord is draw - ing nigh;
strew palms where he ad - vanc - es, spread gar - ments in his way;
his ti - dings of sal - va - tion to ev - ery peo - ple bring,
his ev - er - last - ing king - dom is light and joy and love;

the right-eous King of glo - ry, fore - told in sa - cred sto - ry.
God's prom-ise fail-eth nev - er, Ho - san - na sound for - ev - er.
who, wait - ing still in sad - ness, would sing his praise with glad - ness.
let us his praise be sound - ing for grace and peace a - bound - ing.

Refrain

O blest is he that came in God the Fa - ther's Name!

text: *Bereden väg för Herren*, Franz M. Franzen, 1812, translated by
Augustus Nelson, *alt.*

76.76.77.66

tune: *Messiah* [Swedish Melody], Swedish melody from the fourteenth century.
Reprinted from the *American Lutheran Hymnal*, by permission of Augsburg
Publishing House.

♩. = 50

Advent

H-109

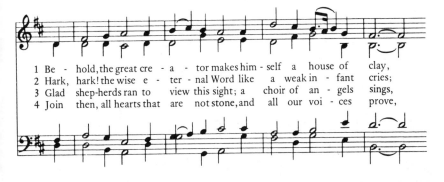

1 Be - hold, the great cre - a - tor makes him - self a house of clay,
2 Hark, hark! the wise e - ter - nal Word like a weak in - fant cries;
3 Glad shep-herds ran to view this sight; a choir of an - gels sings,
4 Join then, all hearts that are not stone, and all our voi - ces prove,

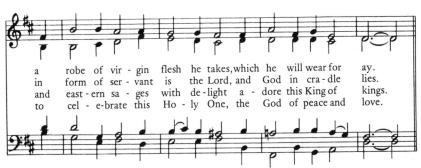

a robe of vir - gin flesh he takes, which he will wear for ay.
in form of ser - vant is the Lord, and God in cra - dle lies.
and east - ern sa - ges with de - light a - dore this King of kings.
to cel - e-brate this Ho - ly One, the God of peace and love.

text: Thomas Pestel, 1559, *alt.*

tune: *This endris nyght*, traditional English melody, harmonized by Ralph
Vaughan Williams. From *The Oxford Book of Carols*, by permission of
Oxford University Press.

8 6.8 6

♩. = 48

Christmas

H-110

1 Fol - low now, this hap - py day, That bright star which
2 The ox, the ass, the qui - et cow Join bright an - gels
3 With hum - ble prayer let us go too And of - fer pre - cious
4 The ti - ny Child from heav'n a - bove is the Pres - ence

leads the way To the low - ly sta - ble where
prais - ing now The Bless - ed Child, our Heav'n - ly King, And
gifts a - new. A faith - ful heart let us be - stow And
of His Love. He brings the Peace of God to earth, So

Lies a Ba - by sweet and fair. Re - joice! Re - joice! For
ev - ery-where the world shall sing Re - joice! Re - joice! For
all the grate-ful love we owe. Re - joice! Re - joice! For
let us join in Christ-mas mirth. Re - joice! Re - joice! Sing

God has come to earth. Christ is born to - day.
God has come to us. Christ is born to - day.
God has sent his Son. Christ is born to - day.
loud your hymns of praise! Christ our Lord is come.

text: Anne Sanders, 1962. © Copyright 1977 by Leslie Bassett. Reprinted by
permission of American Composers Alliance, New York.

tune: *Natale*, Leslie Bassett, 1962. © Copyright 1977 by Leslie Bassett.
Reprinted by permission of American Composers Alliance, New York.

Irr.

♩ = 132

Christmas

H-111

1 From east to west, from shore to shore, let ev - 'ry heart
2 Be - hold, the world's cre - a - tor wears the form and fash -
3 For this how won - drous - ly he wrought! A maid in low -
4 And while the an - gels in the sky sang praise a - bove
5 All glo - ry for this bless - ed morn to God the Fa -

1 a - wake and sing the ho - ly Child whom Ma - ry bore,
2 ion of a slave; our ver - y flesh our Mak - er shares,
3 ly hu - man place be - came, in ways be - yond all thought,
4 the si - lent field, to shep - herds poor the Lord most high,
5 ther ev - er be; all praise to thee, O Vir - gin - born,

1 the Christ, the ev - er last - ing King.
2 his fal - len crea - tures all to save.
3 the cho - sen ves - sel of his grace.
4 the one great shep - herd, was re - vealed.
5 all praise, O Ho - ly Ghost, to thee. A - men.

text: *A solis ortus cardine. Ad usque*, from Coelius Sedulius' *Paean*
        Alphabeticus de Christo, translated by John Ellerton, 1870, *alt.*   88.88

tune: *A solis ortus cardine*, plainsong melody, Mode iii, harmonized by Theodore Marier,
        1977. Harmony, copyright 1978 by The Church Pension Fund. All Rights Reserved.

♩ = 60

Christmas

H-112

Go tell it on the moun - tain, o - ver the hills and ev - 'ry where; Go tell it on the moun - tain that Je - sus Christ is

Last time to ⊕

Christmas

1. 2. 3. *(To Chorus)*   *(Last time only)*

born.   born.

1 Though I was a sin-ner, I prayed both night and day; I
2 When I was a seek-er, I sought both night and day; I
3 He made me a watch-man up - on the cit-y wall, and

asked the Lord to help me, and he showed me the way.
asked my Lord to help me, and he taught me the way.
if I am a Chris-tian, I am the least of all.

D. S.

text: Anonymous American folk hymn, 19th century.   Irr.

tune: *Go Tell It on the Mountain*, American folk tune, arranged and
       harmonized by Hale Smith, 1977. Arrangement and harmonization,
       copyright 1978 by The Church Pension Fund. All Rights Reserved.

♩ = 120

H-113a

1 On this day earth shall ring
2 His the doom, ours the mirth;
3 God's bright star, o'er his head,
4 On this day an - gels sing;

With the song chil - dren sing To the Lord, Christ our King,
When he came down to earth Beth - le - hem saw his birth;
Wise Men three to him led; Kneel they low by his bed,
With their song earth shall ring, Prais - ing Christ, heav - en's King,

Born on earth to save us; Him the Fa - ther gave us.
Ox and ass be - side him From the cold would hide him.
Lay their gifts be - fore him, Praise him and a - dore him.
Born on earth to save us; Peace and love he gave us.

Christmas

Refrain *

Id - e - o - o - o, Id - e - o - o - o,

Id - e - o glo - ri - a in ex - cel - sis De - o!

(♩)

* therefore: Glory to God in the highest!

text: *Personent hodie voces puerulae*, from the *Piae Cantiones* (1582),
translated by Jane M. Joseph, 1924. Copyright by G. Schirmer, Inc.
Used by permission.

666.66 with refrain

tune: *Personent hodie*, melody from the *Piae Cantiones* (1582), harmonized by
Gustav Holst, 1924. Copyright, G. Schirmer, Inc. Used by permission.

♩ = 76

Alternate harmonization, H-113b

H-113b

1 On this day earth shall ring 'earth shall ring With the song chil-dren sing
2 His the doom, ours the mirth; When he came down to earth,
3 God's bright star o'er his head, Wise Men three to him led;
4 On this day an-gels sing; With their song earth shall ring,

To the Lord, Christ our King, Born on earth to save us;
Beth-le-hem saw his birth; Ox and ass be-side him
Kneel they low by his bed, Lay their gifts be-fore him,
Prais-ing Christ, heav-en's King, Born on earth to save us;

*Refrain**

Him the Fa-ther gave us.
From the cold would hide him.
Praise him and a-dore him.
Peace and love he gave us.
Id - e - o - o - o, Id - e - o -

* therefore: Glory to God in the highest!

Christmas

text: *Personent hodie voces puerulae*, from the *Piae Cantiones* (1582),
translated by Jane M. Joseph, 1924. Copyright, G. Schirmer, Inc.
Used by permission.

666.66 with refrain

tune: *Personent hodie*, melody from the *Piae Cantiones* (1582), harmonized by
Richard Proulx, 1978. Harmony, copyright 1978 by Richard Proulx.
Used with his permission.

♩ = 76

Alternate harmonization, H-113a

H-114

1 To - day our God of his great mer - cy hath
2 To - day in Beth - le - hem did be - fall, a
3 To - day there spake an an - gel bright, to
4 There - fore 'tis meet we kneel to - day, and

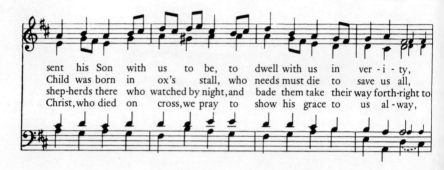

sent his Son with us to be, to dwell with us in ver - i - ty,
Child was born in ox's stall, who needs must die to save us all,
shep-herds there who watched by night, and bade them take their way forth-right to
Christ, who died on cross, we pray to show his grace to us al - way,

God who is our Sav - ior, God who is our Sav - ior.
God who is our Sav - ior, God who is our Sav - ior.
God who is our Sav - ior, to God who is our Sav - ior.
God who is our Sav - ior, God who is our Sav - ior.

text: English Medieval Carol, ca. fifteenth century.

tune: *Kent Carol*, medieval English carol, harmonized by Edgar Pettman.
Reproduced by permission of E. Freeman & Co. Ltd., 138-140 Charing
Cross Road, London WC2H OLD

88.86.6

♩ = 84

Christmas

H-115

1 Great God, we sing that might-y hand by which sup-
2 By day, by night, at home, a-broad, still are we
3 With grate-ful hearts the past we own; the fu-ture,
4 In scenes ex-alt-ed or de-pressed thou art our

port-ed still we stand; the o-p'ning year thy
guard-ed by our God: by his in-cess-ant
all to us un-known, we to thy guard-ian
joy, and thou our rest; thy good-ness all our

mer-cy shows; let mer-cy crown it till it close.
boun-ty fed, by his un-err-ing coun-sel led.
care com-mit, and, peace-ful, leave be-fore thy feet.
hopes shall raise, a-dored through all our chang-ing days.

text: Philip Doddridge, 1755, *alt.*   88.88
tune: *Wareham*, William Knapp, 1738   ♩ = 96

New Year

H-116

1 When Christ's ap - pear - ing was made known, King He - rod
2 The east - ern sa - ges saw from far and fol - lowed
3 With - in the Jor - dan's sa - cred flood the heaven - ly
4 O what a mir - a - cle di - vine, when wa - ter
5 All glo - ry, Je - sus, be to thee for this thy

1 trem - bled for his throne; but he who of - fers heaven - ly
2 on his guid - ing star; by light their way to Light they
3 Lamb in meek-ness stood, that he, to whom no sin was
4 red - dened in - to wine! He spake the word, and forth it
5 glad e - piph - a - ny: whom with the Fa - ther we a -

Epiphany

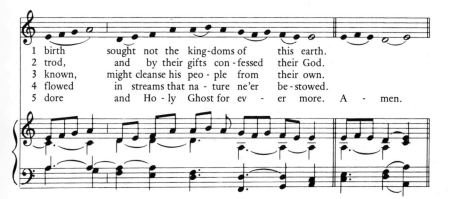

1 birth	sought not the	king-doms of		this earth.	
2 trod,	and by their	gifts con - fessed		their God.	
3 known,	might cleanse his	peo - ple from		their own.	
4 flowed	in streams that	na - ture ne'er		be - stowed.	
5 dore	and Ho - ly	Ghost for ev	-	er more.	A - men.

Stanzas 1, 2, and 5 would be appropriate on the Epiphany.

Stanzas (1), 3, and 5 would be appropriate on the First Sunday after the Epiphany.

Stanzas (1), 4 and 5 would be appropriate on the Second Sunday after the Epiphany when the Gospel is the Wedding at Cana.

text: *Hostis Herodes impie,* from Coelius Sedulius' *Paean Alphabeticus de Christo,* translated by John M. Neale and The Compilers of *The Hymnbook of the Anglican Church of Canada and the United Church of Canada,* alt.   88.88

tune: *Hostis Herodes impie,* plainsong melody, Mode iii, harmonized by Theodore Marier, 1976. Harmony, copyright 1978 by The Church Pension Fund. All Rights Reserved.   ♩ = 60

Alternate tunes, *Erhalt uns, Herr,* H-117; *Spires,* The Hymnal, No. 61

H-117

1 When Christ's ap - pear - ing was made known, King He - rod
2 The east - ern sa - ges saw from far and fol - lowed
3 With - in the Jor - dan's sa - cred flood the heaven - ly
4 O what a mir - a - cle di - vine, when wa - ter
5 All glo - ry, Je - sus, be to thee for this thy

1 trem - bled for his throne; but he who of - fers heaven -
2 on his guid - ing star; by light their way to light
3 Lamb in meek - ness stood, that he, to whom no sin
4 red - dened in - to wine! He spake the word, and forth
5 glad e - piph - a - ny: whom with the Fa - ther we

1 ly birth sought not the king - doms of this earth.
2 they trod, and by their gifts con - fessed their God.
3 was known, might cleanse his peo - ple from their own.
4 it flowed in streams that na - ture ne'er be - stowed.
5 a - dore and Ho - ly Ghost for ev - er more.

Stanzas 1, 2, and 5 would be appropriate on the Epiphany.

Stanzas (1), 3, and 5 would be appropriate on the First Sunday after the Epiphany.

Stanzas (1), 4, and 5 would be appropriate on the Second Sunday after the Epiphany when the Gospel is the Wedding at Cana.

text: *Hostis Herodes impie*, from Coelius Sedulius' *Paean Alphabeticus de Christo*, translated by John M. Neale and The Compilers of *The Hymnbook of the Anglican Church of Canada and the United Church of Canada*, alt.

88.88

tune: *Erhalt uns, Herr*, melody from the *Geistliche Leider* (Wittenberg, 1543), harmonized by Russell Schulz-Widmar, 1978. Harmony, copyright, 1978 by The Church Pension Fund. All Rights Reserved.

♩ = 52

Alternate tunes, *Hostis Herodes, impie*, H-116; *Spires*, The Hymnal, No. 61

Epiphany

H-118a

1 The	sin	- less	one	to	Jor	- dan	came,	and	in	the
2 Up	- ris	- ing	from	the	wa	- ters	there,	the	voice	from
3 A	- bove	him	see	the	heaven	- ly	Dove,	the	sign	of
4 How	blest	that	mis	- sion	then	be	- gun	to	heal	and
5 O	Christ,	your	sons	bap	- tized	from	sin,	go	forth	with
6 On	you	may	all	your	peo	- ple	feed,	and	know	you

1 riv	- er	shared	our	stain;	God's	right	- eous	- ness	he
2 heaven	true	wit	- ness	bare	that	Christ,	the	Son	of
3 God	the	Fa	- ther's	love,	now	by	the	Ho	- ly
4 save	a	race	un	- done! Straight	to	the	wil	- der
5 you	a	world	to	win:	grant	them	the	Ho	- ly
6 are	the	Bread	in	- deed,	who	gives	e	- ter	- nal

1 thus	ful	- filled,	and	chose	the	path	his	Fa	- ther willed.
2 God,	had	come	to	lead	his	scat	- tered	peo	- ple home.
3 Spir	- it	shed	up	- on	the	Son's	a	- noint	- ed head.
4 ness	he	goes	to	wres	- tle	with	his	peo	- ple's foes.
5 Spir	- it's	power	to	shield	them	in	temp	- ta	- tion's hour.
6 life	to	those	that	with	you	died,	and	with	you rose.

play organ

text: George B. Timms, from *English Praise* by permission of Oxford University Press. 88.88

tune: *Solemnis haec festivitas,* melody from the *Paris Gradual* (1685), harmonized by Arthur Hutchings, from *English Praise* by permission of Oxford University Press.

♩ = 44

Alternate harmonization, H-118b

The First Sunday After the Epiphany

H-118b

1 The sin - less one to Jor - dan came, and in the
2 Up - ris - ing from the wa - ters there, the voice from
3 A - bove him see the heaven - ly Dove, the sign of
4 How blest that mis - sion then be - gun to heal and
5 O Christ, your sons bap - tized from sin, go forth with
6 On you may all your peo - ple feed, and know you

1 riv - er shared our stain; God's right - eous - ness he
2 heaven true wit - ness bare that Christ, the Son of
3 God the Fa - ther's love, now by the Ho - ly
4 save a race un - done! Straight to the wil - der -
5 you a world to win: grant them the Ho - ly
6 are the Bread in - deed, who gives e - ter - nal

1 thus ful - filled, and chose the path his Fa - ther willed.
2 God, had come to lead his scat - tered peo - ple home.
3 Spir - it shed up - on the Son's a - noint - ed head.
4 ness he goes to wres - tle with his peo - ple's foes.
5 Spir - it's power to shield them in temp - ta - tion's hour.
6 life to those that with you died, and with you rose.

The First Sunday After the Epiphany

text: George B. Timms, from *English Praise* by permission of Oxford
       University Press.

tune: *Solemnis haec festivitas*, melody from the *Paris Gradual* (1685),
       harmonized by Gerre Hancock, 1978. Harmony, copyright 1978
       by The Church Pension Fund. All Rights Reserved.

Alternate harmonization, H-118a

88.88

H-119

1 When Je - sus went to Jor - dan's stream his Fa - ther's will o -
2 The Ho - ly Spir - it then was shown, a dove on him de -
3 He came by wa - ter and by blood to heal our lost con -

bey - ing, and was bap - tized by John, there came a
scend - ing; so Tri - une God is here made known in
di - tion; he cleans - es rec - on - ciles to God, and

voice from heav - en say - ing, "This is my dear be -
Christ as love un - end - ing. He taught, he healed, he
gives the Great Com - mis - sion. Then let us not heed

lov - ed Son up - on whom rests my fa - vor." And
raised the dead, yet, in his great en - deav - or to
world - ly lies nor rest up - on our mer - it, but

The First Sunday After the Epiphany

till God's will is ful-ly done he will not bend or
save us, his own blood was shed; but death could hold him
trust in Christ who will bap-tize with wa - ter and the

wa - ver, for he is Christ the Sav - ior.
nev - er. He rose, and lives for ev - er.
Spir - it that we may life in - her - it.

text: *Christ unser Herr zum Jordan kam*, Martin Luther, 1541, paraphrased
by F. Bland Tucker, 1977. Paraphrase, copyright 1978 by The Church
Pension Fund. All Rights Reserved.   87.87.87.87 7

tune: *Christ unser Herr zum Jordan kam*, German melody as it appears in
Johann Sebastian Bach's *371 Chorales*.   ♩ = 84

H-120

1 Christ, when for us you were bap - tized, God's
2 God called you his be - lov - ed Son, called
3 Straight - way and stead - fast un - til death you
4 Bap - tize us with your Spir - it, Lord, your

Spir - it on you came, as peace - ful as a
you his ser - vant too; his king - dom you were
then o - beyed his call free - ly as Son of
cross on us be signed, that, like - wise in God's

Dove and yet as ur - gent as a flame.
called to preach, his ho - ly will to do.
Man to serve and give your life for all.
ser - vice we may per - fect free - dom find. A - men.

text: F. Bland Tucker, 1977. Text, copyright 1978 by The Church Pension Fund.
All Rights Reserved.
tune: *Caithness*, melody in *Scottish Psalter* (1635)

8.6.8.6
♩ = 88

The First Sunday After the Epiphany

H-121

1 Christ up - on the moun-tain peak⌣ stands a - lone in glo - ry
2 Trem - bling at his feet we saw⌣ Mo - ses and E - li - jah
3 Swift the cloud of glo - ry came. God pro-claim - ing in the
4 This is God's be - lov - ed Son! Law and proph-ets fade be -

blaz - ing; let us, if we dare to speak,
speak - ing. All the proph - ets and the law⌣
thun - der⌣ Je - sus as his Son by name!
fore him; first and last and on - ly One,

with the saints and an - gels praise him.
shout through him their joy - ful greet - ing. ⎫
Na - tions cry a - loud in won - der ⎬ Al - le - lu - ia!
let cre - a - tion now a - dore him! ⎭

text: Brian Wren, 1962. By permission of Oxford University Press.

tune: *Shillingford*, Peter Cutts. By permission of Oxford University Press.

Alternate tune, *Mowsley*, H-122

78.78.4

♩ = 72

The Last Sunday After the Epiphany

H-122

1 Christ up - on the moun-tain peak stands a - lone in
2 Trem-bling at his feet we saw Mo - ses and E -
3 Swift the cloud of glo - ry came: God pro - claim - ing
4 This is God's be - lov - ed Son! Law and proph-ets

glo - ry blaz - ing; let us, if we dare to speak,
li - jah speak-ing. All the proph - ets and the law
in the thun - der Je - sus as his Son by name!
fade be - fore him; first and last and on - ly One,

with the saints and an - gels praise him.
shout through him their joy - ful greet - ing. } A - le - lu - ia!
Na - tions cry a - loud in won - der
let cre - a - tion now a - dore him!

text: Brian Wren, 1962. By permission of Oxford University Press.   78.78.4

tune: *Mowsley*, Cyril V. Taylor, from the *BBC Hymnbook* by permission of
Oxford University Press.   o = 66

Alternate tune, *Shillingford*, H-121

The Last Sunday After the Epiphany

H-123

1 Wilt thou for-give that sin, where I be - gun, which
2 Wilt thou for-give that sin, by which I won oth -
3 I have a sin of fear that when I have spun my

is my sin, though it were done be - fore? Wilt thou for-give those
ers to sin, and made my sin their door? Wilt thou for-give that
last thread,I shall per - ish on the shore; swear by thy-self, that

sins through which I run and do run still, though still I
sin which I did shun a year or two, but wal - lowed
at my death thy Son shall shine as he shines now, and

do de-plore? When thou hast done,thou hast not done, for I have more.
in a score? When thou hast done,thou hast not done, for I have more.
here - to-fore. And hav -ing done that, thou hast done, I fear no more.

text: John Donne, from *Poems* (1633).

10 10.10 10.8 4

tune: *So giebst du*, melody from the *Geist und Lehr-reiches Kirchen und
Haus Buch* (Dresden, 1694), second line slightly adapted, with harmony
from Johann Sebastian Bach.

♩ = 80

Alternate tunes *Donne*, H-124a,b

Lent

H-124a

1 Wilt thou for-give that sin, where I be - gun, which is my sin, though it were done be - fore? Wilt thou for-give those sins through which I run and do run still, though still I do de - plore?

2 Wilt thou for-give that sin by which I won oth - ers to sin, and made my sin their door? Wilt thou for-give that sin which I did shun a year or two, but wal-lowed in a score?

3 I have a sin of fear that when I have spun my last thread, I shall per - ish on the shore; swear by thy-self, that at my death thy Son shall shine as he shines now, and here - to - fore.

Lent

When thou hast done, thou hast not done, for I have more.
When thou hast done, thou hast not done, for I have more.
And hav-ing done that, thou hast done, I fear no more.

text: John Donne, from *Poems* (1633).

10 10.10 10.84

tune: *Donne*, melody and bass by John Hilton, realization by Elizabeth Poston.
© Elizabeth Poston 1967, from *The Cambridge Hymnal*, all rights controlled by Cambridge University Press. Used by permission.

♩ = 80

Alternate version, H-124b; alternate tune, *So giebst du*, H-123

H-124b

1 Wilt thou for-give that sin, where I be - gun, which is my sin, though
2 Wilt thou for-give that sin by which I won oth - ers to sin, and
3 I have a sin of fear that when I have spun my last thread, I shall

it were done be - fore? Wilt thou for-give those sins through which I
made my sin their door? Wilt thou for-give that sin which I did
per - ish on the shore; swear by thy-self, that at my death thy

run and do run still, though still I do de - plore?
shun a year or two, but wal-lowed in a score?
Son shall shine as he shines now, and here - to - fore.

Lent

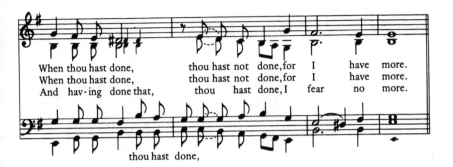

text: John Donne, from *Poems* (1633).

10 10.10 10.84

tune: *Donne*, melody and bass by John Hilton, realization by Elizabeth Poston. © Elizabeth Poston, 1967, from *The Cambridge Hymnal*, all rights controlled by Cambridge University Press. Used by permission.

♩ = 80

Alternate version, H-124a; alternate tune, *So giebst du*, H-123

H-125

Lent

1 Come, let us fol - low where our Cap-tain trod, our
2 Led on their way by this tri - um-phant sign, the
3 Each new - born ser - vant of the Cru - ci - fied bears
4 O Lord, once lift - ed on the glo - rious tree, as
5 So shall our song of tri - umph ev - er be: praise

Repeat Refrain

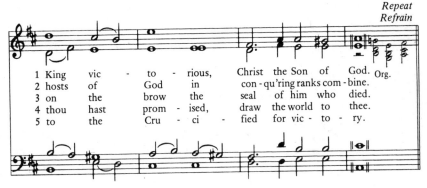

1 King vic - to - rious, Christ the Son of God. Org.
2 hosts of God in con - qu'ring ranks com - bine.
3 on the brow the seal of him who died.
4 thou hast prom - ised, draw the world to thee.
5 to the Cru - ci - fied for vic - to - ry.

text: George W. Kitchin and Michael R. Newbolt, *alt.* By permission of
The Proprietors of *Hymns Ancient and Modern.*

tune: *Crucifer*, Sidney H. Nicholson, 1916. By permission of The Proprietors
of *Hymns Ancient and Modern.*

10 10 with refrain

♩ = 96

H-126

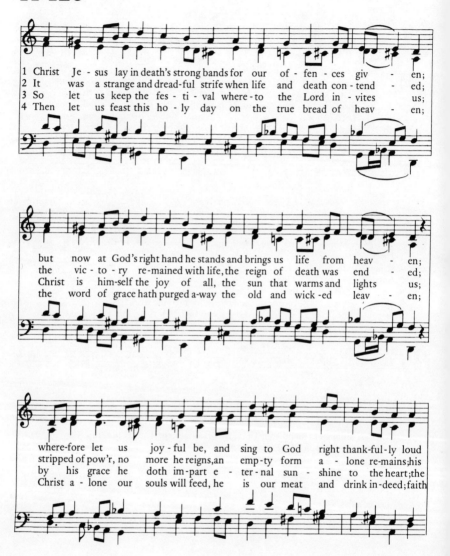

1 Christ Je - sus lay in death's strong bands for our of - fen - ces giv - en;
2 It was a strange and dread-ful strife when life and death con - tend - ed;
3 So let us keep the fes - ti - val where - to the Lord in - vites us;
4 Then let us feast this ho - ly day on the true bread of heav - en;

but now at God's right hand he stands and brings us life from heav - en;
the vic - to - ry re - mained with life, the reign of death was end - ed;
Christ is him-self the joy of all, the sun that warms and lights us;
the word of grace hath purged a-way the old and wick -ed leav - en;

where-fore let us joy - ful be, and sing to God right thank-ful-ly loud
stripped of pow'r, no more he reigns, an emp-ty form a - lone re-mains; his
by his grace he doth im-part e - ter-nal sun - shine to the heart; the
Christ a - lone our souls will feed, he is our meat and drink in-deed; faith

Easter

songs of al - le - lu - ia! Al - le - lu - ia!
sting is lost for ev - er! Al - le - lu - ia!
night of sin is end - ed! Al - le - lu - ia!
lives up - on no oth - er! Al - le - lu - ia!

text: *Christ lag in Todesbanden*, Martin Luther, 1524, translated by
Richard Massie, 1854, *alt.*   87. 87. 78 with alleluia

tune: *Christ lag in Todesbanden*, medieval German melody based on *Victimae Paschali*, adapted and harmonized by Johann Sebastian Bach, 1740.   ♩ = 66

H-127

1 Christ is a - ris - en from the grave's dark pris - on. So let our joy rise full and free: Christ our com - fort true will be. Al - le - lu - ia!

2 Were Christ not a - ris - en then death were still our pris - on. Now, with him to life re - stored, we

Easter

praise the Fa - ther of our Lord. Al - le - lu - ia!

3 Al - le - lu - ia! Al - le - lu - ia!

Al - le - lu - ia! Now let our joy rise full and free:

Christ our com - fort true will be. Al - le - lu - ia!

The tune is based on Victimae Paschali, No. 97, *in* The Hymnal. *The two hymns can be sung in alternation between two groups. One group (choir, or perhaps soloist(s) sings the* Victimae *in D, pausing after Stanzas 3, 7, and 8. At these points, another group (congregation or choir) sings successive thirds of* Christ is erstanden.

text: *Christ ist erstanden von der Marter alle,* anonymous German hymn, based on *Victimae Paschali,* from the *Geistlich Lieder* (1535), translated by Martin Seltz. Adapted from the text taken from *The Worship Supplement,* © 1969 by Concordia Publishing House. Used by permission.

tune: *Christ is erstanden,* medieval German folk song, harmonized by Russell Schultz-Widmar, 1978. Harmony, copyright 1978 by The Church Pension Fund. All Right Reserved.

Irr.

♩ = 56

H-128

1 Christ the Lord is risen a - gain, Christ hath bro - ken
2 He who bore all pain and loss, once re - ject - ed
3 He who went down to the grave is ex - alt - ed

ev - 'ry chain! Hark, an - gel - ic voi - ces cry,
on the cross, lives in glo - ry now on high,
now to save; now through Chris - ten - dom it rings

sing - ing ev - er - more on high: ⎱
pleads for us and hears our cry: ⎰ Al - le - lu - ia!
that the Lamb is King of kings: ⎰

Easter

text: *Christus ist erstanden*, Michael Weiss, 1531, translated by Catherine
        Winkworth, 1858, *alt*.   77.77.4

tune: *Orientis partibus*, medieval French melody, harmonized by Alastair
        Cassels-Brown, 1978. Harmony, copyright 1978 by The Church
        Pension Fund. All Rights Reserved.   ♩ = 88

Alternate tune, *Christ ist erstanden*, H-129

H-129

1 Christ the Lord is risen a-gain, Christ hath bro-ken ev-'ry chain!
2 He who bore all pain and loss, once re-ject-ed on the cross,
3 He who went down to the grave is ex-alt-ed now to save;

Hark, an-gel-ic voi-ces cry, sing-ing ev-er-more on high:
lives in glo-ry now on high, pleads for us and hears our cry:
now through Chris-ten-dom it rings that the Lamb is King of kings:

Al-le-lu - ia. Al - le - lu - ia. Al - le - lu -

Easter

After stanza 3.

text: *Christus ist erstanden*, Michael Weiss, 1531, translated by Catherine
Winkworth, 1858, *alt.*

tune: *Christ is erstanden*, medieval German melody, harmonized by Richard
Proulx, 1978. Harmony, copyright 1978 by Richard Proulx.
Used with his permission.

Alternate tune, *Orientis partibus*, H-128

77.77.4

♩ = 56

H-130

1 Chris - tians, haste your vows to pay, Al - le - lu - ia!
2 For the sheep the Lamb hath bled, Al - le - lu - ia!
3 Christ, the Vic - tim un - de - filed, Al - le - lu - ia!
4 Christ, who once for sin - ners bled, Al - le - lu - ia!
*5 Hail, e - ter - nal hope on high! Al - le - lu - ia!

1 for the Lord is risen to - day; Al - le - lu - ia!
2 sin - less in the sin - ner's stead; Al - le - lu - ia!
3 God and world hath rec - on - ciled, Al - le - lu - ia!
4 now the first - born from the dead, Al - le - lu - ia!
5 Hail, thou King of vic - to - ry! Al - le - lu - ia!

1 of - fer ye your prais - es meet, Al - le - lu - ia!
2 Christ is risen, to - day we cry, Al - le - lu - ia!
3 while in strange and aw - ful strife, Al - le - lu - ia!
4 throned in end - less might and power, Al - le - lu - ia!
5 Hail, thou Prince of life a - dored! Al - le - lu - ia!

Easter

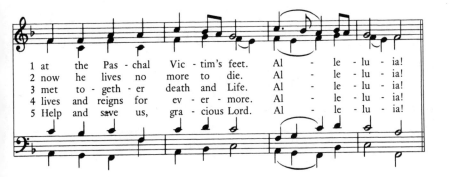

1 at	the	Pas - chal	Vic - tim's feet.	Al - le - lu - ia!
2 now	he	lives no	more to die.	Al - le - lu - ia!
3 met	to - geth - er	death and Life.	Al - le - lu - ia!
4 lives	and	reigns for	ev - er - more.	Al - le - lu - ia!
5 Help	and	save us,	gra - cious Lord.	Al - le - lu - ia!

text: *Victimae Paschali laudes*, Latin sequence hymn, translated by
     Jane E. Leeson, 1851, *alt.*

77.77 with alleluias

tune: *Llanfair*, melody by Robert Williams, 1817, harmonized by Alec Wyton, 1977.
     Harmony, copyright 1978 by The Church Pension Fund. All Rights Reserved.

♩ = 56

Alternate harmonization, The Hymnal, No. 104²

H-131

1 Come a - way to the skies, my be - lov - ed, a - rise and re-
2 Now with sing - ing and praise, let us spend all the days, by
3 For the glo - ry we were first cre - at - ed to share, both the
4 We with thanks do ap - prove the de - sign of that love which hath
*5 Hal - le - lu - jah we sing, to our Fa - ther and King, and his

Capo up 1 A   D   A

1 joice in the day thou wast born; on this fes - ti - val day, come ex-
2 heav - en - ly Fa - ther be - stow'd, while his grace we re - ceive from his
3 na - ture and king-dom di - vine! Now cre - at - ed a - gain that our
4 join'd us to Je - sus' Name; so u - nit - ed in heart, let us
5 rap - tur - ous prais - es, re - peat: to the Lamb that was slain, hal - le-

D   E7   A   A7   D   Em

1 ult - ing a - way, and with sing - ing to Zi - on re - turn.
2 boun - ty, and live to the hon - or and glo - ry of God.
3 lives may re - main, through-out time and e - ter - ni - ty thine.
4 nev - er more part, till we meet at the feast of the Lamb.
5 lu - jah a - gain, sing, all heav - en, and fall at his feet.

A7   Em   A7   D   G   D

Easter

Keyboard and guitars may sound together for good effect.

text: Anonymous, from the *Southern Harmony* (1835), *alt.*   12 9.12 9

tune: *Middlebury*, American folk melody, harmonized by Alastair Cassels-Brown, 1977.
        Harmony, copyright 1978 by The Church Pension Fund. All Rights Reserved.   ♩ = 108

H-132

1 Good Chris - tians all, re - joice and sing! Now is the
2 The Lord of life is risen to - day! Sing songs of
3 Praise we in songs of vic - to - ry that love, that
4 Your Name we bless, O ris - en Lord, and sing to -

tri - umph of our King! To all the world glad news we bring:
praise a - long his way; let all the earth re - joice and say:
life which can-not die, and sing with hearts up - lift - ed high:
day with one ac - cord the life laid down, the life re - stored:

Refrain

Al - le - lu - ia! Al - le - lu - ia! Al - le - lu - ia!

text: Cyril A. Alington, 1931, *alt*. By permission of The Proprietors of
Hymns Ancient and Modern.   888. with alleluias

tune: *Gelobt sei Gott*, melody from Vulpius' *Ein Schön geistlich Gesangbuch*
(1609), harmony as in *The Pilgrim Hymnal* (1958).   ♩ = 44

Easter

H-133

1 I know that my Re - deem - er lives; what joy the
2 He lives, to bless me with his love; he lives, to
3 He lives, all glo - ry to his Name; he lives, my

blest as - sur - ance gives! He lives, he lives, who
plead for me a - bove; he lives, my hun - gry
Sav - ior, still the same; what joy the blest as

once was dead; he lives, my ev - er - last - ing Head!
soul to feed; he lives, to help in time of need.
sur - rance gives; I know that my Re - deem - er lives!

text: Samuel Medley, 1755, *alt.*
tune: *Duke Street*, John Hatton, 1793.

88.88
♩ = 72

Easter

H-134a

1 Now the green blade ris - eth from the bur - ied grain, wheat that in
2 In the grave they laid him, Love whom men had slain, think - ing that
3 Forth he came at East - er, like the ris - en grain, he that for
4 When our hearts are win - try, griev - ing, or in pain, thy touch can

dark earth man - y days has lain; Love lives a - gain, that with the
nev - er he would wake a - gain, laid in the earth like grain that
three days in the grave had lain; quick from the dead my ris - en
call us back to life a - gain, fields of our hearts that dead and

dead has been:
sleeps un - seen:
Lord is seen: Love is come a - gain like wheat that spring-eth green.
bare have been:

Easter

A drone bass on E and the B below may be added.

text: John M. Crum, from *The Oxford Book of Carols*, by permission of
       Oxford University Press.   11 10.11 10

tune: *Noël Nouvelet*, medieval French carol, harmonized by Alastair
       Cassels-Brown, 1977. Harmonization, copyright 1978 by The Church
       Pension Fund. All Rights Reserved.   ♩ = 72

Alternate harmonization, H-134b

H-134b

Introduction (Flute)

Verse 1

Now the green blade ris - eth from the bur - ied grain,

wheat that in dark earth man-y days has lain;

Love lives a - gain, that with the dead has been:

Love is come a - gain like wheat that spring-eth green.

Easter

Verse 2

In the grave they laid him, Love whom men had slain,

(Violin)

pizz.

(Cello)

think - ing that nev - er he would wake a - gain,

(Flute)

(Vln.)

laid in the earth like grain that sleeps un - seen:

Love is come a - gain like wheat that spring-eth green.

Verse 3

Forth he came at East - er, like the ris - en grain,

(Fl.)

(Vln.)

(arco)

he that for three days in the grave had lain;

quick from the dead my ris - en Lord is seen:

Love is come a - gain like wheat that spring-eth green.

Verse 4

When our hearts are win - try, griev - ing, or in pain,

thy touch can call us back to life a - gain;

fields of our hearts that dead and bare have been:

Love is come a - gain like wheat that spring-eth green.

text: John M. Crum, from *The Oxford Book of Carols*, by permission of
Oxford University Press.

tune: *Noël Nouvelet*, medieval French carol, arranged and harmonized by
Alastair Cassels-Brown, 1977. Arrangement and harmony, copyright, 1978
by The Church Pension Fund. All Rights Reserved.

Alternate harmonization, H-134a

11 10.11 10

♩ = 72

H-135

1 On earth has dawned this day of days, where - on the faith - ful
2 The ser - pent's craft, sin, death, and hell, this day be - fore the
3 At ear - ly morn, with spic - es rare, the wom - en three as -
4 "Whom seek ye here?" the an - gel said; "He ris - en is, he
5 So let our songs to heav - en wing, the vault with al - le -

1 give God praise! For Christ is ris - en from the tomb, and
2 con - queror fell: all suf - fering, sor - row, ill, the Name of
3 sem - bled there, all to a - noint fair Mar - y's Son, who
4 is not dead; see where he lay; let joy be - gin, the
5 lu - ias ring, in praise of him; our ris - en Lord, to

1 light and joy have con - quered doom.
2 Je - sus ris'n this day o'er - came.
3 o - ver death had vic - tory won. } Al - le - lu - ia!
4 tomb is emp - ty: en - ter in!"
5 all sal - va - tion doth af - ford.

text: *Erscheinen ist der herrlich Tag*, Nikolaus Herman, 1560, Stanzas 1, 3,
and 5, translated by Charles S. Terry, 1929, *alt.*, from
Bach's Four-part Chorals, by permission of Oxford University Press.
Stanza 2 translated by Arthur T. Russell, 1851.   88.88.4

tune: *Erscheinen ist der herrlich Tag*, melody by Nikolaus Herman, 1560,
harmonized by Gotthart Erthräus, 1608.   ♩. = 40

Easter

H-136

1 The Lamb's high ban - quet called to share, ar - rayed in
2 Pro - tect - ed in the Pas - chal night from the de -
3 Now Christ our Pass - o - ver is slain, the Lamb of
4 O all - suf - fi - cient Sac - ri - fice, be - neath thee
5 All praise be thine, O ris - en Lord, from death to

1 gar - ments white and fair, the Red Sea past, we fain would
2 stroy - ing an - gels' might, in tri - umph went the ran - somed
3 God with - out a stain; his flesh, the true un - leav - ened
4 hell de - feat - ed lies; thy cap - tive peo - ple are set
5 end - less life re - stored; all praise to God the Fa - ther

1 sing to Je - sus our tri - umph - ant King.
2 free from Phar - aoh's cru - el tyr - an - ny.
3 bread, is free - ly of - fered in our stead.
4 free, and end - less life re - stored in thee.
5 be and Ho - ly Ghost e - ter - nal - ly. A - men.

Easter

text: *Ad coenam Agni providi*, anonymous Latin hymn, translated by John M. Neale, 1851, and others. 88.88

tune: *Ad coenam Agni providi*, plainsong melody, Mode viii, harmonized by Theodore Marier, 1977. Harmonization, copyright 1978 by The Church Pension Fund. All Rights Reserved. ♩ = 60

Alternate tune, *Deus tuorum militum* [Grenoble], H-137

H-137

1 The Lamb's high ban - quet called to share, ar - rayed in
2 Pro - tect - ed in the pas - chal night from the de -
3 Now Christ our Pass - o - ver is slain, the Lamb of
4 O all - suf - fi - cient Sac - ri - fice, be - neath thee
5 All praise be thine, O ris - en Lord, from death to

1 gar - ments white and fair, the Red Sea past, we fain would
2 stroy - ing an - gel's might, in tri - umph went the ran - somed
3 God with - out a stain; his flesh, the true un - leav - ened
4 hell de - feat - ed lies; thy cap - tive peo - ple are set
5 end - less life re - stored; all praise to God the Fa - ther

1 sing to Je - sus our tri - um - phant King.
2 free from Phar - aoh's cru - el tyr - an - ny.
3 bread, is free - ly of - fered in our stead.
4 free, and end - less life re - stored in thee.
5 be and Ho - ly Ghost e - ter - nal - ly. A - men.

text: *Ad coenam Agni providi*, anonymous Latin hymn, translated by John M.
Neale, 1851, and others.   88.88

tune: *Deus tuorum militum* [Grenoble], melody from the *Grenoble
Antiphoner* (1753).   ♩. = 50

Alternate tune, *Ad coenam Agni providi*, H-136; this harmonization available
in a lower key in The Hymnal, No. 344

Easter

H-138

1 Through the Red Sea brought at last, al - le - lu - ia,
2 Like the cloud that o - ver - head, al - le - lu - ia,
3 In that cloud and in that sea, al - le - lu - ia,

E - gypt's chains be - hind we cast, al - le - lu - ia. Deep and wide
through the bil - lows Is - rael led, al - le - lu - ia, by his tomb
bur - ied and bap - tized were we, al - le - lu - ia. Earth - ly night

flows the tide sev - 'ring us from bond - age past, al - le - lu - ia!
Christ makes room, souls re - stor - ing from the dead, al - le - lu - ia!
brought us light which is ours e - ter - nal - ly, al - le - lu - ia!

Keyboard and guitars should not sound together.

text: Ronald A. Knox, 1939. Used by permission of Burns & Oates, 2-10 Jerdan Place, London SW6 5PT.

tune: *Straf mich nicht*, melody from *Hundert Arien* (1694), harmonized by Alastair Cassels-Brown, 1977. Harmony, copyright 1978 by The Church Pension Fund. All Rights Reserved.

77.33.7

♩ = 60

Easter

H-139

1 This joy - ful East - er - tide, a - way with sin and
2 My flesh in hope shall rest, and for a sea - son
3 Death's flood hath lost his chill, since Je - sus crossed the

sor — — row! My Love, the Cru - ci -
slum — — ber, till trump from east to
riv — — er: Lord of all life, from

Refrain

fied, hath sprung to life this mor — — row.
west shall wake the dead in num — — ber. } Had
ill my pass - ing life de - liv — — er.

Christ, that once was slain, ne'er burst his three day pris -

Easter

on,   our   faith had   been in   vain;   but   now hath Christ a-

ris - en,   a - ris - en,   a - ris - en,   a-

ris - - - - en.

text: George R. Woodward, 1902, *alt*. By permission of
A.R. Mowbray & Co., Ltd.

tune: *Vreuchten* [Dutch carol], melody from David's *Psalmen* (1685), harmonized
by Charles Wood. By permission of A.R. Mowbray & Co., Ltd.

6 7.6 7 with refrain

♩ = 60

H-140

1 A hymn of glo - ry let us sing, new hymns through-
2 You are a pres - ent joy, O Lord; you will be
3 O ris - en Christ, as - cend -ed Lord, all praise to

out the world shall ring; by a new way none ev - er trod
ev - er our re - ward; and great the light in you we see
you let earth ac - cord, who are, while end-less ag - es run,

Christ takes his place—the throne of God!
to guide us to e - ter - ni - ty.
with Fa - ther and with Spir - it, One. A - men.

text: *Hymnum canamus Domino (gloriae)*, The Venerable Bede, Stanzas 1
and 2 translated by Elizabeth R. Charles, 1858, *alt.*, Stanza 3
translated by Benjamin Webb, 1854, *alt.*

88.88

tune: *Christe redemptor*, plainsong melody, Mode i, harmonized by C. Winfred
Douglas. Harmonization by permission of The Church Pension Fund.

♩ = 60

Alternate tune, *Agincourt Hymn* [Deo gratias], H-141

Ascension

H-141

1 A hymn of glo - ry let us sing, new hymns through -
2 You are a pres - ent joy, O Lord; you will be
3 O ris - en Christ, as - cend - ed Lord, all praise to

out the world shall ring; by a new way- none
ev - er our re - ward; and great the light in
you let earth ac - cord, who are, while end - less

ev - er trod, Christ takes his place — the throne of God!
you we see to guide us to e - ter - ni - ty.
ag - es run, with Fa - ther and with Spir - it, One.

text: *Hymnum canamus Domino (gloriae)* The Venerable Bede, Stanzas 1 and 2 translated by Elizabeth R. Charles, 1858, *alt.*, Stanza 3 translated by Benjamin Webb, 1854, *alt.*

tune: *Agincourt Hymn* [Deo gratias], English melody, ca. 1415, arrangement as in *Hymnal for Colleges and Schools* (1956), edited by E. Harold Geer. Used by permission of Yale University Press.

Alternate tune, *Christe redemptor*, H-140

88.88

♩. = 52

Ascension

H-142

1 Christ, a-bove all glo-ry seat-ed! King e-ter-nal, strong to save!
2 There thy king-doms all a-dore thee, heaven a-bove and earth be-low,
3 So when thou a-gain in glo-ry on the clouds of heaven shalt shine,

Dy-ing, thou hast death de-feat-ed; bur-ied, thou hast spoiled the grave.
while the depths of hell be-fore thee trem-bling and de-feat-ed bow.
we, thy flock, may stand be-fore thee, owned for ev-er-more as thine.

Thou art gone, where now is giv-en what no mor-tal might could gain:
We, O Lord, with hearts a-dor-ing, fol-low thee a-bove the sky:
Hail! all hail! In thee con-fid-ing, Je-sus, thee shall all a-dore,

Ascension

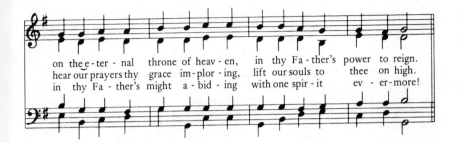

on the e - ter - nal throne of heav - en, in thy Fa - ther's power to reign.
hear our prayers thy grace im - plor - ing, lift our souls to thee on high.
in thy Fa - ther's might a - bid - ing with one spir - it ev - er - more!

text: *Aeterne Rex altissime, Redemptor*, medieval Latin hymn, translated by
James Woodford, 1852.

8 7.8 7.D

tune: *Jesu, meines Lebens Leber* [Alle Menschen müssen Sterben], melody from
the *Kirchengesangbuch* (Darmstadt, 1687).

♩ = 46

H-143

1 O Lord most high, e - ter - nal King, by thee
2 As - cend - ing to the Fa - ther's throne thou claim'st
3 Be thou our joy, O might - y Lord, as thou
4 O ris - en Christ, as - cend - ed Lord, all praise

re - deemed thy praise we sing. The bonds of death are
the king - dom as thine own; and an - gels won - der
wilt be our great re - ward; let all our glo - ry
to thee let earth ac - cord, who art, while end - less

burst by thee, and grace has won the vic - to - ry.
when they see how changed is our hu - man - i - ty.
be in thee both now and through e - ter - ni - ty.
ag - es run, with Fa - ther and with Spir - it one.

Ascension

text: *Aeterne Rex altissime, Redemptor*, medieval Latin hymn, translated
by F. Bland Tucker, 1977. Translation, copyright 1978 by The Church
Pension Fund. All Rights Reserved.

88.88

tune: *Aeterne Rex altissime*, plainsong melody, Mode viii, arranged and
harmonized by James H. Arnold, from the *English Hymnal*, by permission
of Oxford University Press.

♩ = 60

Alternate tune, *Gonfalon Royal*, H-144

H-144

1 O   Lord most high, e - ter - nal King,   by thee re -
2 As - cend - ing to   the   Fa - ther's throne   thou claim'st the
3 Be   thou our joy, O   might - y   Lord,   as thou wilt
4 O   ris - en Christ, as - cend - ed Lord,   all praise to

deemed thy praise we   sing.   The   bonds of death   are
king - dom as   thine   own,   and   an - gels won - der
be   our great re -   ward;   let   all   our glo - ry
thee   let earth ac - cord,   who   art, while end - less

burst   by   thee,   and   grace has won   the   vic - to - ry.
when they see   how   changed is   our   hu - man - i - ty.
be   in   thee both   now   and through e - ter - ni - ty.
ag - es   run, with   Fa - ther and with   Spir - it one.

Ascension

text: *Aeterne Rex altissime, Redemptor*, medieval Latin hymn, translated by   88.88
        F. Bland Tucker, 1977. Translation, copyright 1978 by The Church
        Pension Fund. All Rights Reserved.

tune: *Gonfalon Royal*, Percy Carter Buck, by permission of
        Oxford University Press. $\lrcorner = 60$

Alternate tune, *Aeterne Rex altissime*, H-143

H-145

1 To thee, O Comfort-er divine, for
2 To thee, whose faithful love had place in
3 To thee, whose faithful power doth heal, en-
4 To thee, by Jesus Christ sent down, of

all thy grace and power benign,
God's great covenant of grace,
lighten, sanctify and seal,
all his gifts the sum and crown,

⎫
⎬ sing we
⎭

al-le-lu-ia, al-le-lu-ia!

text: Frances R. Havergal, 1872, *alt.*

tune: *St. Bartholomew's*, David McK. Williams, 1977. Music, copyright 1978 by the Church Pension Fund. All Rights Reserved.

88.10

♩ = 60

Pentecost

H-146a

1 Come down, O Spir-it, Love Di-vine, and fill the hearts that
2 We beg you, Ho-ly Com-fort-er, to check the rush of
3 Bap-tis-mal grace brought you to dwell in mor-tal tem-ples,
4 As Par-a-clete you com-fort us, O Gift of God, sent
5 Through you a-lone can we per-ceive the Fa-ther and his

1 you have made; con-vert, trans-form and pur-i-
2 pas-sion's fires, to melt the steel of hard-ened
3 hearts of clay; de-pose the i-dols throned there-
4 by our Lord; e-ter-nal fount of burn-ing
5 on-ly Son; and you, their vi-brant bond of

1 fy the lives of all who ask your aid.
2 hearts, to fill our wills with pure de-sires.
3 in and prompt us by your grace to pray.
4 zeal, life's heal-ing unc-tion and re-ward.
5 love, in per-sons three, in God-head one. A-men.

This is the Veni Creator Spiritus, *which is one
of the two alternative hymns required in the ordination rite of the Prayer Book,
pp. 520, 533, and 544.*

text: *Veni Creator Spiritus, Mentes tuorum visita,* attributed to Rabanus
  Maurus, translated by Frank Quinn, 1975, *alt.* Copyright, 1975
  by St. Rose Priory. Used by permission.

tune: *Old Hundredth,* Louis Bourgeois, 1551

Alternate harmonization with fauxbourdon, H-146b

8 8.8 8
♩ = 50

Pentecost

H-146b

1 Come down, O Spir - it, Love Di - vine, and fill the hearts that
2 We beg you, Ho - ly Com - fort - er, to check the rush of
3 Bap - tis-mal grace brought you to dwell in mor - tal tem - ples,
4 As Par - a - clete you com - fort us, O Gift of God, sent
5 Through you a - lone can we per - ceive the Fa - ther and his

1 you have made; con - vert, trans-form and pur - i -
2 pas - sion's fires, to melt the steel of hard - ened
3 hearts of clay; de - pose the i - dols throned there -
4 by our Lord; e - ter - nal fount of burn - ing
5 on - ly Son; and you, their vi - brant bond of

1 fy the lives of all who ask your aid.
2 hearts, to fill our wills with pure de - sires.
3 in and prompt us by your grace to pray.
4 zeal, life's heal - ing unc - tion and re - ward.
5 love, in per - sons three, in God - head one. A - men.

Pentecost

The melody is in the tenor.

This is the Veni Creator Spiritus, *which is one of the two alternative hymns required in the ordination rite of the Prayer Book, pp. 520, 533, and 544.*

text: *Veni Creator Spiritus, Mentes turoum visita*, attributed to Rabanus
        Maurus, translated by Frank Quinn, 1975, *alt.* Copyright, 1975
        by St. Rose Priory. Used by permission

tune: *Old Hundredth*, Louis Bourgeois, 1551; fauxbourdon by John Dowland.

Alternate harmonization, H-146a

8 8.8 8

♩ = 50

H-147

1 Come, Ho - ly Ghost, God and Lord!
2 Thou ho - ly Light, guide di - vine,
3 Thou ho - ly Fire, com - fort true,

Be all thy gra - cious gifts out - poured
Oh, cause the word of life to shine!
grant us the will thy work to do

on each be - liev - er's mind and heart;
Teach us to know our God a - right
and in thy ser - vice to a - bide;

thy fer - vent love to each im - part.
and call him Fa - ther with de - light.
let tri - als turn us not a - side.

Pentecost

Lord, by the bright - ness of thy light,
From ev - ery er - ror keep us free;
Lord, by thy power pre - pare each heart

thou in the faith dost all u - nite
let none but Christ our Mas - ter be
and to our weak - ness strength im - part

of ev-ery land and ev-ery tongue; this to thy praise, O Lord,
that we in liv-ing faith a - bide, in him, our Lord, with all
that brave-ly here we may con - tend, through life and death to thee,

our God be sung. }
our might con - fide. } Hal - le - lu - jah! Hal - le - lu - jah!
our Lord, as - cend. }

text: *Komm, Heiliger Geist, Herre Gott,* Martin Luther, 1524.
        From *The Lutheran Hymnal,* © 1941 by Concordia Publishing House, *alt.*
        Used by permission.   78.88.88.8 10 with alleluias

tune: *Komm, Heiliger Geist,* as in the *Enchiridion* (Erfurt, 1524)

♩ = 63

H-148

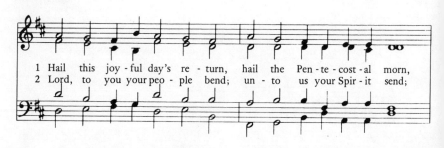

1 Hail this joy - ful day's re - turn, hail the Pen - te - cost - al morn,
2 Lord, to you your peo - ple bend; un - to us your Spir - it send;

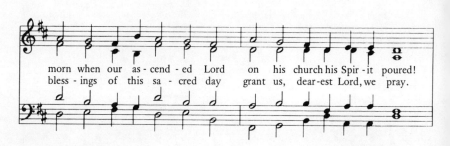

morn when our as - cend - ed Lord on his church his Spir - it poured!
bless - ings of this sa - cred day grant us, dear - est Lord, we pray.

Like to clo - ven tongues of flame on the twelve the Spir - it came —
You who did our fa - thers guide, with their chil - dren still a - bide;

tongues, that earth may hear their call, fire, that love may burn in all.
grant us par - don, grant us peace, till our earth - ly wan - d'rings cease.

text: *Beata nobis gaudia*, attributed to Hilary of Poitiers, translated by
        Robert Campbell,1830, *alt*. Used by permission of Burns & Oates,
        2-10 Jerdan Place, London SW6 5PT   77.77.D

tune: *Goudimel 75*, Claude Goudimel, 1562, adapted and harmonized by
        Russell Schulz-Widmar, 1978. Adaptation and harmonization,
        Copyright, 1978 by The Church Pension fund. All Rights Reserved.   ♩ = 63

Alternate tune, *Ives*, H-149

H-149

1 Hail this joy-ful day's re-turn, hail the Pen - te - cost - al morn;
2 Lord, to you your peo-ple bend; un - to us your Spir - it send;

morn when our as - cend-ed Lord on his church his Spir - it poured!
bless - ings of this sa-cred day grant us, dear - est Lord, we pray.

Like to clo -ven tongues of flame on the twelve the Spir - it came —
You who did our fa - thers guide, with their chil - dren still a - bide;

tongues, that earth may hear their call, fire, that love may burn in all.
grant us par - don, grant us peace, till our earth-ly wan-d'rings cease.

text: *Beata nobis gaudia*, attributed to Hilary of Poitiers, translated by
Robert Campbell, 1830, *alt.* Used by permission of Burns & Oates,
2-10 Jerdan Place, London SW6 5PT

tune: *Ives*, as it appears in *The Plymouth Collection of Hymns and Tunes* (1855).

77.77.D

♩ = 50

Alternate tune, *Goudimel 75*, H-148

Pentecost

H-150

1 Ho - ly Spir - it, font of light, fo - cus of God's glo - ry bright,
Fa - ther of the fa - ther-less, giv - er of gifts lim - it - less,

shed on us a shin - ing ray. 2 Source of strength and sure re - lief,
come and touch our hearts to - day. On our jour - ney grant us aid,

com - fort - er in time of grief, en - ter in and be our guest.
fresh-ening breeze and cool - ing shade, in our la - bor in - ward rest.

Pentecost

3 En - ter each as - pir - ing heart, oc - cu - py its in - most part
All that gives to us our worth, all that ben - e - fits the earth,

with your daz-zling pur - i - ty. 4 With your soft, re - fresh - ing rains
you bring to ma - tu - ri - ty. Shake with rush - ing wind our will;

break our drought, re - move our stains; bind up all our in - jur - ies.
melt with fire our i - cy chill; bring to light our per - jur - ies.

5 As your prom-ise we be-lieve, make us read - y to re-ceive
Grant en-ab-ling en-er-gy, cour-age in ad-ver-si-ty,

gifts from your un-bound-ed store.
joys that last for-ev-er-more. A - men.

This is the Veni Sancte Spiritus, *which is one of
the two alternative hymns required in the ordination rite of the Prayer Book,
pp. 520, 533, and 544.*

text: *Veni Sancte Spiritus*, anonymous Latin hymn, ca. 1200, translated by
John Webster Grant. *alt.* Copyright by John Webster Grant. Used by
permission of John Webster Grant.   77.77.77

tune: *The Golden Sequence*, plainsong melody, Mode i, harmonized by C. Winfred
Douglas. Harmonization used by permission of The Church Pension Fund.   ♩ = 60

Alternate tune, *Webb*, H-151

H-151

1 Ho - ly Spir - it, fount of light, fo - cus of God's glo - ry bright,
2 Source of strength and sure re - lief, com - fort - er in time of grief,
3 En - ter each as - pir - ing heart, oc - cu - py its in-most part
4 With your soft, re - fresh - ing rains break our drought, re - move our stains;
5 As your prom - ise we be - lieve, make us read - y to re - ceive

1 shed on us a shin - ing ray. Fa - ther of the fa - ther - less,
2 en - ter in and be our guest. On our jour - ney grant us aid,
3 with your daz - zling pur - i - ty. All that gives to us our worth,
4 bind up all our in - jur - ies. Shake with rush - ing wind our will;
5 gifts from your un - bound - ed store. Grant en - ab - ling en - er - gy,

1 giv - er of gifts lim - it - less, come and touch our hearts to - day.
2 fresh-ening breeze and cool-ing shade, in our la - bor in - ward rest.
3 all that ben - e - fits the earth, you bring to ma - tu - ri - ty.
4 melt with fire our i - cy chill; bring to light our per - jur - ies.
5 cour - age in ad - ver - si - ty, joys that last for ev - er-more. A - men.

Pentecost

This is the Veni Sancte Spiritus *which is one of*
the two alternative hymns required in the ordination rite of the Prayer Book,
pp. 520, 533, and 544.

text: *Veni Sancte Spiritus*, anonymous Latin hymn, ca 1200, translated by
    John Webster Grant, *alt.* Copyright by John Webster Grant. Used by
    permission of John Webster Grant.

tune: *Webb*, Samuel Webb, 1782.

Alternate tune, *The Golden Sequence*, H-150

77.77.77

♩ = 48

H-152

1 Up - on that Whit-sun morn - ing a sound from heav-en came,
2 In Sa - lem's street was gath - ered a crowd from many a land,
3 Then come, all Chris - tian peo - ple, keep fes - ti - val to - day,

and filled the place of meet - ing with rush - ing wind and flame:
and all in their own tongues did the Gos - pel un - der - stand:
for God the Ho - ly Spir - it dwells with his Church for ay:

what Christ had prom - ised now oc - curred as each A - pos - tle
for by the tri - umph of the Son the curse of Ba - bel
and grieve him not, O Chris - tian soul, his grace with - in shall

Pentecost

spoke the word be - neath the Spir-it's thun - der, and to the ears of
was un-done when God did send the Spir - it; and to the bless-ed
make you whole in bod - y, mind and spir - it, un - til you reach the

all who heard pro - claimed sal - va - tion's won - der.
Three in One be hon - or, praise and mer - it.
prom-ised goal, a king-dom to in - her - it.

Keyboard and guitar should not sound together.

text: George B. Timms. From *English Praise* by permission of
       Oxford University Press.

tune: *Song of the Holy Spirit*, Dutch melody, ca. 1860, harmonized by
       Alastair Cassels-Brown, 1977. Harmony, copyright 1978 by The Church
       Pension Fund. All Rights Reserved.

76.76.88 7.87

♩ = 126

H-153

1 O Holy Spir - it, by whose breath
2 You are the seek - er's sure re - source,
3 In you God's en - er - gy is shown;
4 Flood our dull sens - es with your light;
5 From in - ner strife grant us re - lease;

1 life ris - es vi - brant out of death;
2 of burn - ing love the liv - ing source,
3 to us your var - ied gifts make known.
4 in mu - tual love our hearts u - nite.
5 turn na - tions to the ways of peace.

1 come to cre - ate, re - new, in - spire;
2 pro - tect - or in the midst of strife,
3 Teach us to speak, teach us to hear;
4 Your pow'r the whole cre - a - tion fills;
5 To full - er life your peo - ple bring

Pentecost

1 come, kin - dle in our hearts your fire.
2 the giv - er and the Lord of life.
3 yours is the tongue and yours the ear.
4 con - firm our weak, un - cer - tain wills.
5 that as one bod - y we may sing:

6 Praise to the Fa - ther, Christ, his Word,

and to the Ho - ly Spir - it: God the Lord. A - men.

This is the Veni Creator Spiritus, *which is one of the two alternative*
hymns required in the ordination rite of the Prayer Book, pp. 520, 533, and 544.

text: *Veni Creator Spiritus*, attributed to Rabanus Maurus, translated by
John Webster Grant, *alt.* Copyright by John Webster Grant. Used by
permission of John Webster Grant.   88.88

tune: *Veni Creator*, plainsong melody, Mode viii, harmonized by Theodore Marier, 1977.
Harmony, copyright 1978 by The Church Pension Fund. All Rights Reserved.

Alternate tune, *Komm, Gott Schöpfer*, H-154   ♩ = 60

H-154

1 O Ho - ly Spir - it, by whose breath life
2 You are the seek - er's sure re - source, of
3 In you God's en - er - gy is shown, to
4 Flood our dull sen - ses with your light; in
5 From in - ner strife grant us re - lease; turn
6 Praise to the Fa - ther, Christ, his Word, and

1 ris - es vi - brant out of death; come to cre - ate, re - new, in -
2 burn - ing love the liv - ing source, pro - tect - or in the midst of
3 us your var - ied gifts make known. Teach us to speak, teach us to
4 mu - tual love our hearts u - nite. Your pow'r the whole cre - a - tion
5 na - tions to the ways of peace. To full - er life your peo - ple
6 to the Spir - it; God the Lord, to whom all hon - or, glo - ry,

1 spire; come, kin - dle in our hearts your fire.
2 strife, the giv - er and the Lord of life.
3 hear; yours is the tongue and yours the ear.
4 fills; con - firm our weak, un - cer - tain wills.
5 bring that as one bod - y we may sing:
6 be both now and for e - ter - ni - ty. A - men.

Pentecost

This is the Veni Creator Spiritus, *which is one of the two alternative hymns required in the ordination rite of the Prayer Book, pp. 520, 533, and 544.*

text: *Veni Creator Spiritus*, attributed to Rabanus Maurus, translated by John Webster Grant, *alt*. Copyright by John Webster Grant. Used by permission of John Webster Grant.

tune: *Komm, Gott Schöpfer*, from Johann Walther's *Chorgesangbuch* (1625)

Alternate tune, *Veni Creator Spiritus*, H-153

88.88

♩ = 50

H-155

1 The an - gel Ga - bri - el from heav - en came, his
2 "For known a bless - ed Moth - er thou shalt be, all
3 Then gen - tle Ma - ry meek - ly bowed her head, "To
4 Of her, Em-man - u - el, the Christ, was born in

wings as drift - ed snow, his eyes as flame;
gen - er - a - tions laud and hon - or thee,
me be as it pleas - eth God," she said,
Beth - le - hem, all on a Christ - mas morn,

"All hail," said he, "thou low - ly maid - en Ma - ry,
thy Son shall be Em-man - u - el, by seers fore - told,
"my soul shall laud and mag - ni - fy his Ho - ly Name."
and Chris - tian folk through-out the world will ev - er say -

most high-ly fa - vor'd la - dy," Glo - ri - a!
most high-ly fa - vor'd la - dy," Glo - ri - a!
Most high-ly fa - vor'd la - dy, Glo - ri - a!
"Most high-ly fa - vor'd la - dy," Glo - ri - a!

Annunciation

text: Sabine Baring-Gould.

tune: *Gabriel's Message* [Basque Carol], a Basque carol harmonized by Edgar
        Pettman. Reproduced by permission of E. Freeman & Co., 138-140
        Charing Cross Road, London WC2H OLD

10 10.12 10

♩. = 66

H-156a

1 The Christ whom earth and sea and sky a-
2 Blest in the mes - sage Ga - briel brought; blest
3 O Lord, the Vir - gin - born, to thee e -

dore and laud and mag - ni - fy, whose might they own, whose
in the work the Spir - it wrought; most blest, to bring to
ter - nal praise and glo - ry be, whom with the Fa - ther

praise they tell, in Ma - ry's bod - y deigned to dwell.
hu - man birth the long De - sired of all the earth.
we a - dore and Ho - ly Spir - it ev - er - more.

Annunciation

text: *Quem terra, pontus, aethera,* Venantius Fortunatus, translated by John
        M. Neale and the Compilers of *Hymns Ancient and Modern, alt.*
        By permission of The Proprietors of *Hymns Ancient and Modern.*   88.88

tune: *Solothurn,* Swiss melody from *Sammlung von Schweitzer Kuhreihen und
        Volksliedern* (1826), harmonized by Alastair Cassels-Brown, 1977.
        Harmony, copyright 1978 by The Church Pension Fund. All Rights Re-
        served.   ♩ = 104

Alternate harmonization, H-156b

Alternate tune, *Quem terra, pontus, aethera,* H-157

H-156b

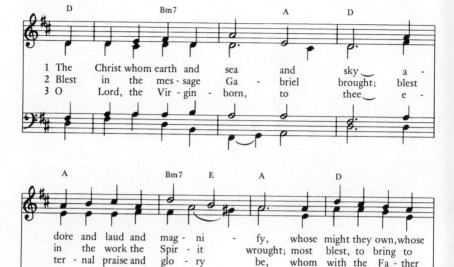

1 The Christ whom earth and sea and sky a-
2 Blest in the mes-sage Ga - briel brought; blest
3 O Lord, the Vir-gin - born, to thee e-

dore and laud and mag - ni - fy, whose might they own, whose
in the work the Spir - it wrought; most blest, to bring to
ter - nal praise and glo - ry be, whom with the Fa - ther

praise they tell, in Ma - ry's bod - y deigned to dwell.
hu - man birth, the long De - sired of all the earth.
we a - dore and Ho - ly Spir - it ev - er - more.

text: *Quem terra, pontus, aethera*, Venantius Fortunatus, translated by John
M. Neale and *The Compilers of Hymns Ancient and Modern, alt*.
By permission of The Proprietors of *Hymns Ancient and Modern*.   88.88

tune: *Solothurn*, Swiss melody from *Sammlung von Schweitzer Kuhreihen und
Volkssliedern* (1826), harmonized by Alastair Cassels-Brown, 1977.
Harmony, copyright 1978 by The Church Pension Fund. All Rights Reserved. ♩ = 104

Alternate harmonization, H-156a

Alternate tune, *Quem terra, pontus, aethera*, H-157

Annunciation

H-157

1 The Christ whom earth and sea and sky a - dore and
2 Blest in the mes - sage Ga - briel brought; blest in the
3 O Lord, the Vir - gin - born, to thee e - ter - nal

laud and mag - ni fy, whose might they own, whose
work the Spir - it wrought; most blest, to bring to
praise and glo - ry be, whom with the Fa - ther

praise they tell, in Ma - ry's bod - y deigned to dwell.
hu - man birth the long De - sired of all the earth.
we a - dore and Ho - ly Spir - it ev - er - more.

text: *Quem terra, pontus, aethera*, Venantius Fortunatus, translated by John
M. Neale and The Compilers of *Hymns Ancient and Modern, alt.*
By permission of The Proprietors of *Hymns Ancient and Modern.*   88.88

tune: *Quem terra, pontus, aethera*, plainsong melody Mode ii, harmonized
by Arthur Hutchings. By permission of The Proprietors of *Hymns Ancient and Modern.*
♩ = 60

Alternate tune, *Solothurn*, H-156a,b

Annunciation

H-158

1. Come, pure hearts, in sweet - est meas - ure sing of those who spread the treas-ure in the ho - ly gos - pels shrined; bless - ed ti - dings

Evangelists

of sal - va - tion, peace on earth their proc - la -

ma - tion, love from God to lost man - kind.

2. See the riv - ers four that glad - den,

with their streams, the bet - ter E - den plant - ed

by our Lord most dear; Christ the foun - tain,

these the wa - ters; drink, O Zi - on's sons and

daugh-ters, drink, and find sal - va - tion here.

3. O that we, thy truth con - fess - ing

and thy ho - ly word pos - sess-ing, Je - sus

A   men.

text: *Psallat chorus corde mundo*, Latin sequence hymn, translated by Robert
        Campbell, 1850.   887.887

tune: *Pure Hearts*, Ned Rorem, 1977. Copyright 1977 by Boosey & Hawkes, Inc.
        All Rights Reserved. International Copyright Secured.
        Used by Arrangement.   ♩ = 100

H-159

1 King of the martyrs' noble band, crown of the
2 hear us now as we celebrate faith unde-
3 Dying, through thee they overcame; living, were
4 Glory to God the Father be; glory to

true of every land, strength of the pilgrim
terred by cruel hate; hear and forgive us,
faithful to thy Name. Turn our rebellious
Christ, who set us free; and to the Spirit,

on the way, beacon by night and cloud by day:
for we too are burdened by the wrong we do.
hearts, and thus win a like victory in us.
living flame, glory unceasing we proclaim.

text: *Rex gloriose martyrum*, medieval Latin hymn, translated by John Webster Grant, *alt.*
       Copyright by John Webster Grant. Used by permission of John Webster Grant.   88.88

tune: *Rex gloriose martyrum*, plainsong melody, Mode viii, harmonized by Theodore Marier,
       1976. Harmony, copyright 1978 by The Church Pension Fund. All Rights Reserved.

Alternate tunes, *Rex gloriose*, H-160; *Rex gloriose*, The Hymnal, No. 8²   ♩ = 60

Martyrs

H-160

1 King of the mar - tyrs' no - ble band, crown of the
2 hear us now as we cel - e - brate faith un - de -
3 Dy - ing, through thee they o - ver - came; liv - ing, were
4 Glo - ry to God the Fa - ther be; glo - ry to

true of ev - ery land, strength of the pil - grim on the
terred by cru - el hate; hear and for - give us for we
faith - ful to thy Name. Turn our re - bel - lious hearts, and
Christ, who set us free; and to the Spir - it, liv - ing

way, bea - con by night and cloud by day:
too are bur - dened by the wrong we do.
thus win a like vic - to - ry in us.
flame, glo - ry un - ceas - ing we pro - claim.

text: *Rex gloriose martyrum*, medieval latin hymn, translated by John Webster
Grant, *alt.*, Copyright by John Webster Grant. Used by permission of
John Webster Grant.

88.88

tune: *Rex gloriose*, melody from the *Andernach Gesangbuch* (1608),
harmonized by Alec Wyton, 1978. Harmony, copyright by The Church
Pension Fund. All Rights Reserved.

♩ =60

Alternate harmonization, The Hymnal, No. 8²
Alternate tune, *Rex gloriose martyrum*, H-159

Martyrs

H-161

1 Morn-ing has bro - ken like the first morn - ing, black-bird has
2 Sweet the rain's new fall sun-lit from heav - en, like the first
3 Mine is the sun - light! Mine is the morn - ing born of the

spo - ken like the first bird. Praise for the sing - ing!
dew - fall on the first grass. Praise for the sweet - ness
one light E - den saw play! Praise with e - la - tion,

Praise for the morn - ing! Praise for them spring - ing fresh from the Word!
of the wet gar - den, sprung in com - plete - ness where his feet pass.
praise ev-ery morn - ing, God's re-cre - a - tion of the new day!

text: Eleanor Farjeon, 1931, alt., from *The Children's Bells*,
published by Oxford University Press. Used by permission of David
Higham Associates, Ltd., London.

5 5.5 4.D

tune: *Bunessan*, old Gaelic melody, harmonized by Alastair Cassels-Brown, 1977.
Harmony, copyright 1978 by The Church Pension Fund. All Rights Reserved. ♩. = 50

Morning

H-162

1 O gra - cious Light, Lord Je - sus Christ,
2 Now sun - set comes, but light shines forth,
3 Wor - thy are you of end - less praise,

in you the Fa - ther's glo - ry shone. Im - mor - tal, ho - ly,
the lamps are lit to pierce the night. Praise Fa - ther, Son, and
O Son of God, Life - giv - ing Lord; where - fore you are, through

blest is he, and blest are you, his ho - ly Son.
Spir - it — God who dwells in the e - ter - nal light.
all the earth and in the high - est heaven a - dored.

text: *Phos hilaron*, ancient Greek hymn, translated by F. Bland Tucker, 1976.
Translation, copyright 1978 by The Church Pension Fund.
All Rights Reserved.

8 8.8 8

tune: *Conditor alme*, plainsong melody, Mode vi, harmonized by C. Winfred
Douglas. Harmony by permission of The Church Pension Fund.

♩ = 60

Alternate tune, *Tallis' Canon*, H-163

Evening

H-163

1 O gra - cious Light, Lord Je - sus Christ, in
2 Now sun - set comes, but light shines forth, the
3 Wor - thy are you of end - less praise, O

you the Fa - ther's glo - ry shone. Im - mor - tal, ho - ly,
lamps are lit to pierce the night. Praise Fa - ther, Son, and
Son of God, Life - giv - ing Lord; where - fore you are, through

blest is he, and blest are you, his ho - ly Son.
Spir - it, God who dwells in the e - ter - nal light.
all the earth and in the high - est heaven a - dored.

Evening

text: *Phos hilaron*, ancient Greek hymn, translated by F. Bland Tucker, 1976.
Translation, copyright 1978 by The Church Pension Fund.
All Rights Reserved.

tune: *Tallis' Canon*, Thomas Tallis, ca. 1567.

Alternate tune, *Conditor alme*, H-162

8 8.8 8

$\textstyle\int$ = 80

H-164

1 All who be-lieve and are bap-tized shall see the Lord's sal-va-tion; bap-tized in-to the death of Christ, each is a new cre-a-tion. Through Christ's re-demp-tion we shall stand a-mong the glo-rious heav'n-ly band of ev-ery tribe and na-tion.

2 With one ac-cord, O God, we pray: grant us thy Ho-ly Spir-it; help us in our in-fir-mi-ty through Je-sus' blood and mer-it. Grant us to grow in grace each day that as is prom-ised here we may e-ter-nal life in-her-it.

text: *Enhever som tror og bliver döbt*, Thomas Kingo, 1689, translated by
George T. Rygh, 1909, *alt*. Reprinted from the *Lutheran Hymnary*,
by permission of Augsburg Publishing House.   87.87.88 7

tune: *Es ist da Heil* [St. Paul], melody from the *Enchiridion* (Erfurt, 1524),
harmonized by Alec Wyton, 1978. Harmony, copyright 1978 by The Church
Pension Fund. All Rights Reserved.   ♩ = 60

Alternate tune, *Bohemian Brethren*, H-223

Baptism

H-165

1 Spir - it of God, un - leashed on earth with rush of wind and
2 You came in power the church to fill; O Ho - ly Spir - it,

roar of flame, with tongues of fire saints spread good news; earth,
come a - gain! Raise up new saints from wa - ters deep; let

kin - dling, blazed her loud ac - claim.
new tongues hail the ris - en Lord. A - men.

text: John Arthur, *alt*. Used by permission of the author.

8 8.8 8

tune: *Donata*, Carl Schalk. Reprinted from *Contemporary Worship 4: Hymns for Baptism and Holy Communion*, copyright 1972, permission of Augsburg Publishing House for Inter Lutheran Commission on Worship.

♩ = 96

Baptism

H-166a

1 De-scend, O Spir-it, purg-ing flame, brand us this
2 For-bid us not this sec-ond birth; grant un-to

day with Je-sus' Name! Con-firm our faith, con-sume our
us the great-er worth! Con-script us in your ser-vice,

doubt; sign us as Christ's, with-in, with-out.
Lord; bap-tize all na-tions with your Word. A - men.

Keyboard and guitars should not sound together

text: Scott Francis Brenner, 1969, *alt*. Words copyright © by The Westminster
       Press. From *The Worshipbook – Services and Hymns*. Used by permission.   88.88

tune: *Llef*, Griffith Hugh Jones, 1890, harmonized by Alastair Cassels-
       Brown, 1977. Harmonization copyright 1978 by The Church Pension Fund.
       All Rights Reserved.   ♩. = 46

Alternate harmonization, H-166b.

Baptism

H-166b

Keyboard and guitars should not sound together

text: Scott Francis Brenner, 1969, *alt.* Words copyright © by The Westminster Press. From *The Worshipbook – Services and Hymns.* Used by permission. 88.88

tune: *Llef,* melody by Griffith Hugh Jones, 1890, harmonized by Alastair Cassels-Brown, 1977. Harmony copyright 1978 by The Church Pension Fund. All Rights Reserved.

♩ = 46

Alternate harmonization, H-166a.

Baptism

H-167

1 O Ho - ly Spir - it, en - ter in; a - mong these hearts thy
2 Left to our - selves we shall but stray; O lead us on the
3 Grant that our days, while life shall last, in pur - est ho - li -

work be - gin, thy tem - ple deign to make us; be
nar - row way, with wis - est coun - sel guide us; and
ness be passed; our minds so rule and strength - en that

thou our sun, thou Light di - vine, a - round and in us
give us stead - fast - ness, that we may hence-forth tru - ly
they may rise o'er things of earth, the hopes and joys that

bright - ly shine, to strength and glad - ness wake us.
fol - low thee, what - ev - er woes be - tide us;
here have birth; and if our course thou length - en,

Baptism

Where thou shin-est, life from heav-en there is giv-en;
heal thou gen-tly hearts now bro-ken, give some to-ken
keep thou pure, Lord, from of-fenc-es, heart and sens-es;

we be-fore thee for that pre-cious gift im-plore thee.
thou art near us, whom we trust to light and cheer us.
bless-ed Spir-it, bid us thus true life in-her-it. A-men.

text: *O Heil'ger Geist, kehr bei uns ein*, Michael Schirmer, 1640, translated
by Catherine Winkworth, 1863, *alt.*   887.887.48.48

tune: *Wie schön leuchtet*, [Frankfort], Philip Nicolai, 1599, adapted and
harmonized by Johann Sebastian Bach, 1740.   ♩ = 66

H-168

1 Praise and thanks-giv - ing be to our cre - a - tor, source of this
2 Not our own ho - li - ness, nor that we have striv - en brings us the
3 Come, Ho - ly Spir - it; come in vis - it - a - tion: you are the

bless - ing, Fa - ther, Med - i - a - tor. Bap - tize and make your own
peace which you, O Christ, have giv - en. Bap - tize and set a - part,
truth, our hope and our sal - va - tion. Bap - tize with joy and power;

these who come be - fore you, while we a - dore you.
come, O ris - en Sav - ior, with grace and fa - vor.
give, O Dove de - scend - ing, life nev - er end - ing. A - men.

text: Frank J. Whiteley and the Rev. Harold F. Yardley, *alt.*
Used by permission of the Rev. Harold F. Yardley.

11 11.11 5

tune: *Christe sanctorum*, French Church melody, 1782, harmonized by Alastair
Cassels-Brown, 1977. Harmony copyright 1978 by The Church Pension Fund. ♩ = 56

Alternate harmonization, No. 157², The Hymnal.

Alternate tune, *Oblation,* The Hymnal, No. 205

Baptism

H-169

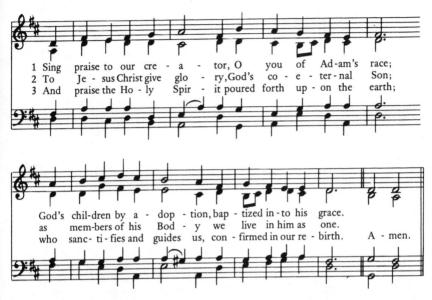

1 Sing praise to our cre - a - tor, O you of Ad-am's race;
2 To Je - sus Christ give glo - ry, God's co - e - ter - nal Son;
3 And praise the Ho - ly Spir - it poured forth up - on the earth;

God's chil-dren by a - dop - tion, bap - tized in - to his grace.
as mem-bers of his Bod - y we live in him as one.
who sanc - ti - fies and guides us, con - firmed in our re - birth. A - men.

text: Mark Evans, *alt.*, © 1961, World Library Publications, Chicago, Il.
Reprinted with Permission, text changed on the advice of
the Theological Committee. 76.76

tune: *Christus, der ist mein Leben* [Christ is my Life],
melody by Melchior Vulpius, 1609.

♩ = 60

Baptism

H-170

1 We know that Christ is raised and dies no more.
2 We share by wa - ter in his sav - ing death.
3 The Fa - ther's splen - dor clothes the Son with life.
4 A new cre - a - tion comes to life and grows

Em - braced by death, he broke its fear - ful hold;
Re - born we share with him an East - er life,
The Spir - it's pow - er shakes the church of God.
as Christ's new bod - y takes on flesh and blood.

1.-3.

and our de - spair he turned to blaz - ing joy.
as liv - ing mem - bers of a liv - ing Christ.
Bap - tized we live with God the Three in One.
The u - ni - verse re - stored and

Baptism

Al - le - lu - ia!
Al - le - lu - ia!
Al - le - lu - ia!

whole will sing: Al - le - lu - ia!

text: John B. Geyer, *alt.* Used by permission of the author.

tune: *Engelberg,* Charles V. Stanford, 1904.

Alternate tune, *Sine nomine,* The Hymnal, No. 126[1]

10 10.10 4

♩ = 60

H-171

1 This is the Spir - it's en - try now: the wa - ter and the word, the cross of Je - sus on your brow, the seal both felt and heard.

2 This mir - a - cle of lives re - born comes from the Lord of breath; the per - fect Man from life was torn, new life comes through his death.

3 Let wa - ter be the sa - cred sign that we must die each day to rise a - gain by his de - sign as fol - l'wers in his way.

4 Re - new - ing Spir - it, we give praise for your bap - tis - mal power that wash - es us through all our days— Lord, cleanse a - gain this hour. A - men.

text: Thomas E. Herbranson, *alt.* Used by permission of the author.

tune: *Perry*, Leo Sowerby. Music copyright © 1964 by Abingdon Press. Used by permission.

8.6.8.6

♩ = 60

Baptism

H-172

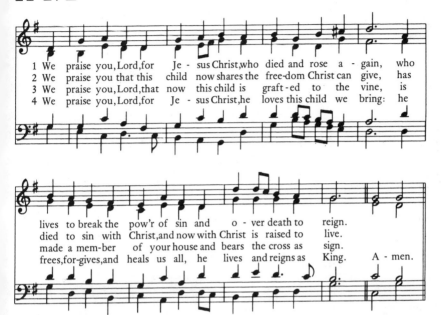

1 We praise you, Lord, for Je - sus Christ, who died and rose a - gain, who
2 We praise you that this child now shares the free-dom Christ can give, has
3 We praise you, Lord, that now this child is graft - ed to the vine, is
4 We praise you, Lord, for Je - sus Christ, he loves this child we bring: he

lives to break the pow'r of sin and o - ver death to reign.
died to sin with Christ, and now with Christ is raised to live.
made a mem-ber of your house and bears the cross as sign.
frees, for-gives, and heals us all, he lives and reigns as King. A - men.

text: Judith R. O'Neill, *alt.* Used by permission of the author.

tune: *St. Magnus*, Jeremiah Clark, 1709.

8 6.8 6

♩ = 108

Baptism

H-173

1 Come, ris - en Lord, and deign to be our
2 We meet as in that up - per room they
3 One bod - y we, one Bod - y who par -
4 One with each oth - er, Lord, for one in

guest; nay, let us be thy guests; the feast is
met; thou at the ta - ble, bless - ing, yet dost
take, one Church u - nit - ed in com - mun - ion
thee, who art one Sav - ior and one liv - ing

thine; thy - self at thine own board make man - i -
stand: "this is my Bod - y;" so thou giv - est
blest; one name we bear, one Bread of life we
Head; then o - pen thou our eyes, that we may

fest in this thy Sac - ra - ment of Bread and Wine.
yet: faith still re - ceives the cup as from thy hand.
break, with all thy saints on earth and saints at rest.
see; be known to us in break - ing of the Bread.

Eucharist

Optional Descant

3 One bod-y we, one Bod-y who par-take, one

Other voices in unison

3 One bod-y we, one Bod-y who par-take, one

Church u-nit-ed in com-mun-ion blest; one name we

Church u-nit-ed in com-mun-ion blest;

bear, one Bread of life we break, with all thy

one name we bear, one Bread of life we break, with

saints on earth and saints at rest. *D. C.*

all thy saints on earth and saints at rest. *D. C.*

text: George Wallace Briggs, 1931, from *Enlarged Songs of Praise* by
permission of Oxford University Press.

tune: *Rosedale*, Leo Sowerby

Alternate tunes, *Edsall* and *Sursum Corda*, The Hymnal, No. 207[1], No. 482[1]

10 10.10 10
♩ = 50

H-174

Piano or Organ*

Gently oscillating, but with body

Organ Pedal

1 Fa - ther, we thank thee
2 Thou, Lord, didst make all
3 Watch o'er thy Church, O
4 As grain, once scat - tered

who hast plant - ed thy ho - ly
for thy pleas - ure, didst give man
Lord in mer - cy, save it from
on the hill - side, was in this

name with - in our hearts. Know-ledge and
food for all his days, giv - ing in
e - vil, guard it still, per - fect it
bro - ken bread made one, so from all

*Tie all repeated notes in hands.

Eucharist

faith and life im - mor - tal Je - sus thy
Christ the bread e - ter - nal; thine is the
in thy love, u - nite it, cleansed and con -
lands thy Church be gath - er'd in - to thy

optional
ending

Son to us im - parts.
power, be thine the praise.
formed un - to thy will.
king - dom by thy Son.

All instruments * * except piano or organ.

sempre con pedale

etc.

sempre tenuto

"OSTINATO" (optional)

text: from the *Didache*, ca. 110, translated by F. Bland Tucker, 1939. Used by permission of The Church Pension Fund. All Rights Reserved.

tune: *Father we thank thee* [Albright], William Albright.
© 1973 Elkan Vogel, Inc. Used by permission.

Alternate tune, *Rendez à Dieu* H-220, The Hymnal, No. 195

98.98

♩ = 60

Suggested Method for Performance

1. Play the 9 pitches in the given order, and in any register (except lower): laissez vibrer.

2. Play steadily in any tempo (mm52-100): each player should choose a different tempo.

3. Starting with the first note only, add one note, in series, to each repetition, i.e., note 1, note 1+2, 1+2+3.........1 to 9.

4. When the complete series is attained, reverse the process, subtracting one pitch at a time from the end of the series, i.e., 1 to 9, 1 to 8.........note 1.

5. When the entire cycle is complete, begin again without interruption.

6. If the interludes are performed, players interrupt their ostinato, returning immediately at the start of the hymn.

7. Instruments should blend as much as possible in order to create an overall "celestial" effect.

**Suggested Instruments

Played by at least three of the following instruments (duplications are possible):

Harp
Glockenspiel
Celesta
Vibraphone
Piano (poss. 4-hand)
Chimes (tub. bells)
Organ Chimes
Glass Harmonica

Handbells
Carillon
Acoustic Guitar (harmonics)
Antique Cymbals (tuned)
Tuned Goblets (arco)
Toy Piano (chrom.)
Prepared Tape (bell or bell-like sounds)
Electric Piano

H-175

1 Com - plet - ed, Lord, the Ho - ly Mys - ter - ies, as
2 Here we have tast - ed in - fi - nite de - lights, be -
3 Through God's good grace these mys - ter - ies are ours, or -

far as lies with - in our mor - tal power! Thy
held a - far that life which soon shall be; O
dained by thee, the ev - er - last - ing Son; blest

death re - mem - bered, feed - ing thus on thee, we
count us wor - thy, Christ, thy joys to share for -
by the Spir - it, breath and flame of life, to

here have known the res - ur - rec - tion hour.
ev - er in e - ter - ni - ty with thee.
whom be praise while end - less ag - es run. A - men.

text: from the Liturgy of St. Basil, translated by Cyril E. Pocknee.
Translation copyright by Cyril E. Pocknee, used by permission.

tune: *Song Four*, Orlando Gibbons, 1623.

10 10.10 10

♩ = 50

Eucharist

H-176

1. For the bread which thou hast bro - ken; For the wine which thou hast poured; For the words which thou hast spo - ken; Now we give thee thanks, O Lord.

2. By this pledge that thou dost love us, By thy gift of peace re - stored, By thy call to heaven a - bove us, Hal-low all our lives, O Lord.

3. With our saint - ed ones in glo - ry Seat - ed at our Fa - ther's board, May the church that wait - eth for thee Keep love's tie un - bro - ken, Lord.

4. In thy ser - vice, Lord, de - fend us. In our hearts keep watch and ward. In the world where thou dost send us Let thy king-dom come, O Lord. A - men.

text: Louis Benson. Used by permission of the estate of Barbara Jefferys.

tune: *Omni Die*, melody from David Corner's *Gross Catolisch Gesangbuch* (1631), setting by William Smith Rockstro.

87.87

♩ = 63

Eucharist

H-177

1 Lord, en - throned in heav'n - ly splen - dor, first be -
*2 Here our hum - blest hom - age pay we, here in
*3 Though the low - liest form doth veil thee as of
4 Pas - chal Lamb, thine of - f'ring fin - ished once for
5 Life im - part - ing heav'n - ly man - na, strick - en

1 got - ten from the dead. Thou a - lone, our strong de -
2 lov - ing rev - 'rence bow; here for faith's dis - cern - ment
3 old in Beth - le - hem, here as there thine an - gels
4 all when thou wast slain. In its full - ness un - di -
5 rock with stream - ing side, heav'n and earth with loud ho -

1 fend - er, lift - est up thy peo - ple's
2 pray we, lest we fail to know thee
3 hail thee, branch and flower of Jes - se's
4 min - ished shall for ev - er more re -
5 san - na wor - ship thee, the Lamb who

Eucharist

1 head. Al - le - lu - ia. Al - le - lu - ia. Al - le -
2 now. Al - le - lu - ia. Al - le - lu - ia. Al - le -
3 stem. Al - le - lu - ia. Al - le - lu - ia. Al - le -
4 main. Al - le - lu - ia. Al - le - lu - ia. Al - le -
5 died. Al - le - lu - ia. Al - le - lu - ia. Al - le -

1 lu - ia. Je - sus, true and liv - ing
2 lu - ia. Thou art here, we ask not
3 lu - ia. We in wor - ship join with
4 lu - ia. Cleans - ing us from ev - 'ry
5 lu - ia. Risen, as - cend - ed, glo - ri -

1 bread! Je - sus, true and liv - ing bread!
2 how. Thou art here, we ask not how.
3 them. We in wor - ship join with them.
4 stain. Cleans - ing us from ev - 'ry stain.
5 fied! Risen, as - cend - ed, glo - ri - fied!

text: George H. Bourne, 1874, *alt.*

tune: *Bryn Calfaria,* melody by William Owen, setting by Theodore A. Beck from *The Worship Supplement,* © 1969 by Concordia Publishing House. Used by permission.

Alternate tune, *Helmsley,* The Hymnal, No. 52

87.87.12 7

♩=69

H-178

1 I come with joy to meet my Lord, for - giv - en, loved, and free,
2 I come with Chris-tians far and near to find, as all are fed,
3 As Christ breaks bread for men to share each proud di - vi - sion ends.
4 And thus with joy we meet our Lord. His pres - ence, al - ways near,
5 To - geth - er met, to - geth-er bound, we'll go our dif - ferent ways,

1 in awe and won - der to re - call his life laid down for me.
2 man's true com - mu - ni - ty of love in Christ's com-mun-ion bread.
3 That love that made us makes us one, and stran-gers now are friends.
4 is in such friend-ship bet - ter known: we see, and praise him here.
5 and as his peo - ple in the world, we'll live and speak his praise.

text: Brian Arthur Wren, 1968. By permission of Oxford University Press.   8 6.8 6

tune: *Land of Rest*, Traditional American melody, collected and harmonized by Annabel Morris Buchanan. Copyright © 1938 by J. Fischer & Bro. Copyright renewed. Used with permission. All Rights Reserved.   ♩. = 50

Eucharist

H-179

1 Dear Fa - ther, in thy house to - day we wait thy kind - ly
2 Blest Spir - it, who with life and light didst quick - en cha - os
3 Great One in Three, in whom are named all fam - i - lies in

love to see. Since thou hast said in truth that they who
to thy praise,whose en - er - gy in sin's de - spite still
earth and heav'n,hear us who have thy prom - ise claimed, and

dwell in love are one in thee, bless those who for thy
lifts our na - ture up to grace: bless those who here pledge
let a wealth of grace be giv'n; grant them in life and

bless - ing wait;their love draw forth and con-se - crate.
their con-sent;Cre - 'a - tor, crown thy sa - cra - ment.
death to be each knit to each, and both to thee. A - men.

text: Robert Hugh Benson, *alt.*   8 8.8 8.88
tune: *Carey* [Surrey], Henry Carey, 1723.   ♩. = 40

Marriage

H-180

1 O thou whose fa - vor hal - lows all oc - ca - sions,
2 Long may they keep the sense of high ad - ven - ture,
3 Al - might - y God, re - deem - er and de - fend - er,

be pres - ent at this cov - e - nant - ing rite;
the gift of joy, the mar - vel of a dream,
be thou their stay what - ev - er may be - tide;

may ev - 'ry pledge of true and last - ing pur - pose
nor ev - er lose the vi - sion as they cher - ish
in - creas - ing - ly may each new year dis - cov - er

be con - se - crat - ed in thy ho - ly sight;
each for the oth - er, hon - or and es - teem;
their lives ma - tured, their mar - riage sanc - ti - fied,

Marriage

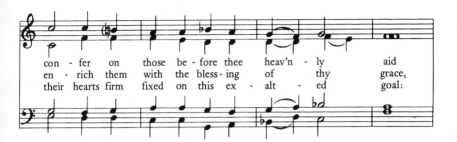

con - fer on those be - fore thee heav'n - ly aid
en - rich them with the bless - ing of thy grace,
their hearts firm fixed on this ex - alt - ed goal:

to keep the sol - emn vows that here are made.
and make their home thy con - stant dwell - ing place.
the praise of God whose name their vows ex - tol.

text: Miriam Drury, from "13 Marriage and Family Hymns" © by The Hymn
Society of America. Used by permission.   11 10.11 10.10 10

tune: *Goudimel 37*, Claude Goudimel, 1562, adapted by David Hurd, 1978.
Adaption copyright 1978 by The Church Pension Fund. All Rights Reserved.   ♩ = 54

H-181

1 O Father blest, we ask of you, we
2 For nei-ther joy nor grief nor place nor
3 O God of love, O Spir-it blest, pre-

ask you, God the Son, to bless those here who now re-
life nor death can part those who, en-joy-ing Je-sus'
serve, in-crease their love; re-main with them, their heav'n-ly

new the vows which made them one. A - men.
grace, in him are one in heart.
guest; pro-tect them from a-bove.

text: Roger Nachtway, stanzas 1 and 3, 1965, Charles Wesley, stanza 2, 1742, *alt*. Copyright 1965 by F.E.L. Publications, Ltd. The selection has been reprinted with permission of the copyright owner, F.E.L. Publications, Ltd., 1925 Pontius Avenue, Los Angeles, CA 90025, Phone: (213)478-0053. Further reproduction is not permitted without written permission of the copyright owner.

8.6.8.6

tune: *St. Mary*, melody from Prys' *Llyfr y Psalmus*, (1621)

♩ = 48

Alternate tune, *Tallis' Ordinal*, The Hymnal, No. 298[1]

Renewal of Marriage Promises

H-182

1 May choirs of an - gels lead you to Par - a - dise on high,
2 And at your com - ing thith - er may you be brought by them
3 As an - gels gave poor Laz - arus from all his ills re - lease,

where dwell the white-robed mar - tyrs who now no more can die.
in - to the ho - ly cit - y, God's true Je - ru - sa - lem.
so may they give you wel - come to ev - er - last - ing peace.

This is a metrical setting of the anthem on pp. 484 and 500 (Rites I and II)
of the Burial Service in the Book of Common Prayer

text: *In paradisum*, anonymous Latin hymn, translated by F. Bland Tucker, 1978.
Translation, copyright 1978 by The Church Pension Fund. All rights reserved. 76.76

tune: *Christus, der ist mein Leben* [Christ is my Life], melody by Melchior
Vulpius, 1609. ♩ = 50

Burial

H-183

Give rest, O Christ, to your ser-vant(s) with your saints, where sor - row and pain are no more, nei - ther sigh - ing, but life ev - er - last - ing. *Fine* You on - ly are im - mor - tal, the cre - a - tor and mak - er of man - kind; and we are mor - tal, form - ed of the earth, and to earth shall we re - turn.

Burial

For so did you or - dain when you cre - a - ted me, say - ing, "You are dust, and to dust you shall re - turn." All of us go down to the dust; yet e - ven at the grave we make our song: al - le - lu - ia, al - le - lu - ia, al - le - lu - ia.

D. C. al Fine

This is a setting of the anthem on pp. 482-3 and 499 (Rites I and II) of the
Burial Service of The Book of Common Prayer

text: from the Russian Orthodox liturgy, translation from The Book of
        Common Prayer (Proposed) © 1977 by Charles Mortimer Guilbert,
        Custodian of the Standard Book of Common Prayer. All rights reserved.
        Used by permission.

tune: *Russian Contakion* [Kieff Melody], from the Russian Orthodox liturgy,
        edited by Walter Parratt.

Irr.

♩ = 56

H-184

Burial

May the choirs of an - gels wel - come you,

and with Laz - a - rus who once was poor

may you have peace ev - er - last - ing.

text: *In paradisum deducant te angeli*, anonymous Latin text. Stanza 1, translation from *The Book of Common Prayer (Proposed)*, © 1977 by Charles Mortimer Guilbert, Custodian of the Standard Book of Common Prayer. All rights reserved. Used by permission.
Stanza 2, translated by Theodore Marier, used with his permission.

Irr.

tune: *In paradisum*, plainsong, Mode vii, harmonized by Theodore Marier, 1977. Harmony, copyright 1978 by The Church Pension Fund. All Rights reserved.

♩ = 60

H-185

Burial

text: *In paradisum deducant te angeli*, anonymous Latin hymn, translated by Paul Ramsey. Used by permission of the translator and The Church Pension Fund.

Irr.

tune: *In paradisum*, plainsong, Mode vii, transcribed and harmonized by Richard Proulx, 1977. Transcription and harmony © 1977 by Richard Proulx, used by his permission.

♩ = 60

Alternate setting, H-186

H-186

Burial

bless your re - pose in ho - ly, ho - ly Je - ru - sa - lem, where the

choirs sing the end - ing of sor - row, e - ter - nal

greet - ing, A - men.

text: *In paradisum deducant te angeli*, anonymous Latin hymn, translated
by Paul Ramsey. Used by permission of the translator and The Church
Pension Fund.

tune: *In paradisum*, Richard Proulx, 1977. Music, © 1977 by Richard Proulx.
Used by permission of the composer.

Alternate setting, H-185

Irr.

♩ = 60

H-187

1 All crea-tures of our God and King, Lift
2 Thou rush-ing wind that art so strong, Ye
3 Thou flow-ing wa - ter, pure and clear, Make
4 Dear moth - er earth, who day by day Un -
5 And all ye men of ten - der heart, For -
6 And thou, most kind and gen - tle death, Wait -
7 Let all things their cre - a - tor bless, And

1 up your voice and with us sing Al - le - lu - ia! Al - le -
2 clouds that sail in heaven a - long, O praise him! Al - le -
3 mu - sic for thy Lord to hear, Al - le - lu - ia! Al - le -
4 fold - est bless-ings on our way, O praise him! Al - le -
5 giv - ing oth - ers, take your part, O sing ye! Al - le -
6 ing to hush our lat - est breath, O praise him! Al - le -
7 wor - ship him in hum - ble - ness, O praise him! Al - le -

General Hymns

1 lu - ia! Thou burn-ing sun with gold-en beam, Thou
2 lu - ia! Thou ris - ing morn, in praise re - joice, Ye
3 lu - ia! Thou fire so mas - ter - ful and bright, Thou
4 lu - ia! The flowers and fruits that in thee grow, Let
5 lu - ia! Ye who long pain and sor - row bear, Praise
6 lu - ia! Thou lead - est home the child of God, And
7 lu - ia! Praise, praise the Fa-ther, praise the Son, And

1 sil - ver moon with soft-er gleam! O praise him, O praise him!
2 lights of eve - ning, find a voice! O praise him, O praise him!
3 giv - est man both warmth and light! O praise him, O praise him!
4 them his glo - ry al - so show! O praise him, O praise him!
5 God and on him cast your care! O praise him, O praise him!
6 Christ our Lord the way hath trod. O praise him, O praise him!
7 praise the Spir - it, Three in One! O praise him, O praise him!

Al - le - lu - ia! Al - le - lu - ia! Al - le - lu - ia!

text: *Laudato sia Dio mio Signore,* Francis of Assisi, translated
by William H. Draper, 1926. Copyright by G. Shirmer, Inc.
Used by permission.   88.44.88 with alleluias

tune: *Lasst uns erfreun* [Vigiles et sancti], melody from *Ausserlesene Catolische Geistliche
Kirchengesange* (1623), harmonized by Ronald Arnatt, 1978. Harmony
copyright 1978 by The Church Pension Fund.   ♩ = 56

Alternate harmonization, The Hymnal, No. 599

H-188

1 All my hope on God is found - ed; he doth still my
2 Pride of man and earth-ly glo - ry, sword and crown be -
3 God's great good-ness aye en-dur - eth, deep his wis - dom
4 Dai - ly doth th'al - might-y Giv - er boun - teous gifts on
5 Still from man to God e - ter - nal sac - ri - fice of

1 trust re - new, Me through change and chance he
2 tray man's trust; What with care and toil he
3 pass - ing thought: Splen - dor, light and life at -
4 us be - stow; His de - sire our soul de -
5 praise be done, High a - bove all prais - es

General Hymns

1 guid - eth, on - ly good and on - ly true. God un -
2 build - eth, tow̧er and tem - ple, fall to dust. But God's
3 tend Him, beau - ty spring - eth out of naught. Ev - er -
4 light - eth, pleas - ure leads us where we go. Love doth
5 prais - ing, for the gift of Christ, his Son. Christ doth

1 known, he a - lone calls my heart to be his own.
2 power, hour by hour, is my tem - ple and my tow̧er.
3 more from his store new-born worlds rise and a - dore.
4 stand at his hand; joy doth wait on his com - mand.
5 call one and all: ye who fol - low shall not fall.

text: Robert Bridges, 1899. From the *Yattendon Hymnal* by permission of
Oxford University Press.

87.87.33 7

tune: *Michael*, Herbert Howells, 1936. Music copyright Novello and Company, Ltd.
Used by permission.

♩ = 120

H-189a

1 As those of old their first fruits brought of vine-yard, flock, and field
2 A world in need now sum-mons us to la - bor, love and give;
3 In grat - i - tude and hum-ble trust we bring our best to thee

to God the giv - er of all good, the source of boun-teous yield;
to make our life an of - fer - ing to God that all may live;
to serve thy cause and share thy love with all hu - man - i - ty.

so we to - day first fruits would bring, the wealth of this good land,
the Church of Christ is call-ing us to make the dream come true:
O thou who gav - est us thy-self in Je - sus Christ thy Son,

General Hymns

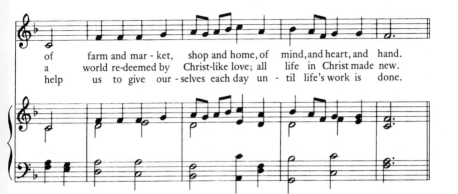

of   farm and mar - ket,   shop and home, of   mind, and heart, and   hand.
a   world re-deemed by   Christ-like love; all   life in Christ made new.
help   us to give our - selves each day un - til life's work is   done.

text: Frank von Christierson, *alt.* 1977, from *Ten Stewardship Hymns*, © 1961
        by the Hymn Society of America. Used by permission.   8 6.8 6.D

tune: *Forest Green*, English traditional melody, harmonized by Robert Powell,
        1977. Harmony copyright 1978 by The Church Pension Fund.   ♩ = 56

Alternate harmonization, H-189b and The Hymnal, No. 21[1].

H-189b

1 As those of old their first fruits brought of vine-yard, flock and field
2 A world in need now sum-mons us to la - bor, love and give;
3 In grat - i - tude and hum-ble trust we bring our best to thee

to God the giv - er of all good, the source of boun-teous yield;
to make our life an of - fer - ing to God that all may live;
to serve thy cause and share thy love with all hu - man - i - ty.

so we to - day first fruits would bring, the wealth of this good land,
the Church of Christ is call - ing us to make the dream come true:
O thou who gav - est us thy-self in Je - sus Christ thy Son,

of farm and mar - ket, shop and home, of mind, and heart, and hand.
a world re-deemed by Christ-like love; all life in Christ made new.
help us to give our - selves each day un - til life's work is done.

text: Frank von Christierson, *alt.* 1977, from *Ten Stewardship Hymns,* © 1961
       by the Hymn Society of America. Used by permission.   8 6.8 6.D

tune: *Forest Green,* English traditional melody, harmonized by Robert Powell,
       1977. Harmony copyright 1978 by the Church Pension Fund.   ♩ = 56

Alternate harmonization, H-189a, and The Hymnal, No. 21².

General Hymns

H-190

1 All glo - ry be to God on high, and peace on earth from
2 O Lamb of God, Lord Je - sus Christ, whom God the Fa - ther
3 You on - ly are the Ho - ly One, who came for our sal -

heav - en, and God's good - will un - fail - ing - ly to
gave us, who for the world was sac - ri - ficed up -
va - tion, and on - ly you are God's true Son, the

all man - kind be giv - en. We bless, we wor - ship you, we raise for
on the cross to save us; and, as you sit at God's right hand, and
first-born of cre - a - tion. You on - ly, Christ, as Lord we own and,

your great glo - ry thanks and praise, O God, Al-might - y Fa - ther.
we for judg - ment there must stand, have mer - cy, Lord, up - on us.
with the Spir - it, you a-lone share in the Fa - ther's glo - ry.

This is a metrical version of the canticle Gloria in excelsis

text: *Allein Gott in der Hoh' sei Ehr'*, Nikolaus Decius, 1522, translated by F. Bland Tucker,
       1977. Translation copyright 1978 by The Church Pension Fund.   87.87.88 7

tune: *Allein Gott in der Hoh'*, attributed to Nikolaus Decius, 1539.   ♩ = 42

General Hymns

H-191

1 Be thou my vi-sion, O Lord of my heart; naught be all
2 Be thou my wis-dom, and thou my true word; I ev-er
3 Rich-es I heed not, nor th' world's emp-ty praise, thou mine in-

else to me, save that thou art— thou my best thought, by
with thee and thou with me Lord; thou my great Fa-ther; thine
her-i-tance, now and al-ways: thou and thou on-ly,

day or by night, wak-ing or sleep-ing, thy pres-ence my light.
own may I be; thou in me dwell-ing, and I one with thee.
first in my heart, high King of heav-en, my treas-ure thou art.

General Hymns

text: *Rob tu mo bhoile, a Comdi cride*, Irish text, ca. 700. Translated by
         Mary Elizabeth Byrne, 1927; versified by Eleanor H. Hull, 1927, *alt.*
         From *The Poem Book of the Gael*: Selected and Edited by Eleanor Hull,
         used by permission of the executors of Miss E. Hull and of Chatto and
         Windus, Ltd.   10 10.9 10

tune: *Slane*, traditional Irish melody, harmonized by Alastair Cassels-
         Brown, 1977. Harmony copyright 1978 by The Church Pension Fund.   ♩ = 108

Alternate harmonization, The Hymnal, No. 122

H-192

1 Bless - ed Je - sus, at thy word we are gath-ered all to
2 All our knowl - edge, sense, and sight lie in deep-est dark-ness
3 Gra - cious Lord, thy - self im - part! Light of light, from God pro -

hear thee; let our hearts and souls be stirred
shroud - ed, till thy Spir - it breaks our night
ceed - ing, o - pen thou our ears and heart,

now to seek and love and fear thee; by thy teach - ings,
with the beams of truth un - cloud - ed; thou a - lone to
help us by thy Spir - it's plead - ing. Hear the cry thy

General Hymns

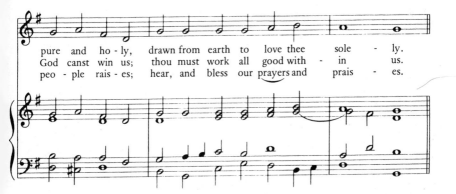

pure and ho - ly, drawn from earth to love thee sole - ly.
God canst win us; thou must work all good with - in us.
peo - ple rais - es; hear, and bless our prayers and prais - es.

text: *Liebster Jesu, wir sind hier*, Tobias Clausnitzer, 1663, translated
        by Catherine Winkworth, 1858.   78.78.88

tune: *Liebster Jesu*, melody by Johann Rudolph Ahle, 1664, harmonized by
        George Herbert Palmer. $o = 42$

H-193

Part
men
unis
women
part

1 Blest be the God of Is - ra - el, the ev - er - liv - ing Lord,
2 Through ho - ly proph-ets did he speak his word to men of old,
3 Of old he swore his sol - emn oath to fa - ther A - bra - ham:
4 O child of prom-ise, you shall be the proph-et of the Lord;
5 The ris - ing Sun shall shine on us to bring the light of day

1 who comes in pow'r to save his own, his peo - ple Is - ra - el.
2 that he would save us from our foes and all who bear us ill.
3 his seed a might-y race should be and blest for ev - er - more.
4 the way of God you shall pre - pare to make his com - ing known.
5 to all who sit in dark - est night and shad-ow of the grave.

1 For Is - ra - el he rais - es up sal - va - tion's tow'r on high
2 So to our fa - thers did he give his cov - en - ant of love;
3 He swore to set his peo - ple free from fear of ev - 'ry foe
4 You shall pro - claim to Is - ra - el sal - va - tion's dawn-ing day,
5 Our foot-steps God shall safe - ly guide to walk the ways of peace.

General Hymns

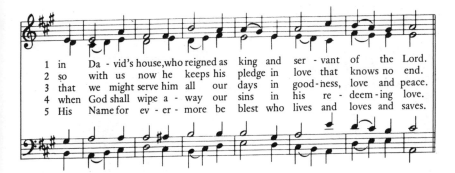

1 in   Da - vid's house, who reigned as king and ser - vant of   the Lord.
2 so   with us   now he   keeps his pledge in love that knows no   end.
3 that we might serve him all   our days in good - ness, love and peace.
4 when God shall wipe a - way our sins in   his   re - deem - ing love.
5 His   Name for ev - er - more be blest who lives and loves and saves.

This is a metrical version of the canticle Benedictus Dominus Deus.

text: James Quinn, 1969, *alt.* From *New Hymns for all Seasons*, copyright
        by Geoffrey Chapman, Ltd. Used by permission.   8 6.8.6 D.

                                                                         ♩ = 60

tune: *St. Matthew*, as in the *Supplement to the New Version*, 1708.

Alternate tune, *Kingsfold*, The Hymnal, No. 101

H-194

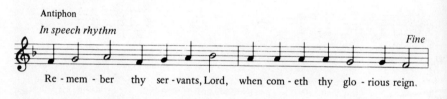

Antiphon

In speech rhythm

Fine

Re - mem - ber thy ser - vants, Lord, when com - eth thy glo - rious reign.

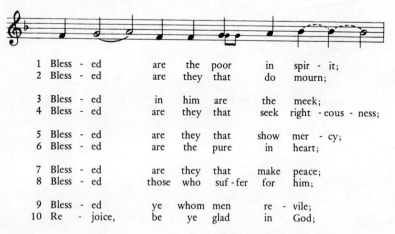

| 1 | Bless - ed | | are | the | poor | in | spir - it; |
| 2 | Bless - ed | | are | they | that | do | mourn; |

| 3 | Bless - ed | | in | him | are | the | meek; |
| 4 | Bless - ed | | are | they | that | seek | right - eous - ness; |

| 5 | Bless - ed | | are | they | that | show | mer - cy; |
| 6 | Bless - ed | | are | the | pure | in | heart; |

| 7 | Bless - ed | | are | they | that | make | peace; |
| 8 | Bless - ed | | those | who | suf - fer | for | him; |

| 9 | Bless - ed | | ye | whom | men | re - vile; |
| 10 | Re - joice, | | be | ye | glad | in | God; |

| 1 | for the heavenly King | - | dom | is | theirs. |
| 2 | for their Lord shall wipe a | - | way | their | tears. |

| 3 | for their heritage shall | | be | the | earth. |
| 4 | in that great day their thirst | | shall | be | quenched. |

| 5 | for God shall be merciful | | un | - to | them. |
| 6 | for in that day shall they | | see | their | God. |

| 7 | for they shall be called chil | - | dren | of | God. |
| 8 | the righteous own the king | - | dom | of | heav'n. |

| 9 | this world shall persecute | | you | for | me. |
| 10 | for in heaven great is | | your | re - | ward. |

text: from the Russian Orthodox liturgy, translated by M.M. Gowen.

tune: *Beatitudes*, from the Russian Orthodox liturgy.

Irr.

♩ = 60

General Hymns

H-195

1 Come, let us join our cheer-ful songs with an-gels round the throne;
  ten thou-sand thou-sand are their tongues, but all their joys are one.

2 'Wor - thy the Lamb that died,' they cry, 'to be ex - alt - ed thus';
  'wor - thy the Lamb,' our lips re - ply, 'for he was slain for us.'

3 Je - sus is wor - thy to re - ceive hon-or and power di - vine;
  may bless-ings, more than we can give, be, Lord, for - ev - er thine.

4 The whole cre - a - tion joins in one to bless the sa - cred Name
  of him that sits up - on the throne, and to a - dore the Lamb.

This is a metrical version of the canticle Dignus es.

text: Isaac Watts, 1707.

tune: *Nun danket all und bringet Ehr* [Graefenberg], Johann Cruger, 1653.

8 6.8 6

♩ = 84

General Hymns

H-196

1 Come, my Way, my Truth, my Life: such a
2 Come, my Light, my Feast, my Strength: such a
3 Come, my Joy, my Love, my Heart: such a

way as gives us breath; such a truth as ends all
light as shows a feast; such a feast as mends in
joy as none can move; such a love as none can

strife; such a life as kill—————eth death.
length; such a strength as makes his guest.
part; such a heart as joys in love.

text: George Herbert.

tune: *The Call*, Ralph Vaughan Williams, from *Five Mystical Songs* (1911).
© Copyright by Stainer & Bell Ltd. All Rights Reserved. Used by permission of Galaxy Music Corp., N.Y., sole U.S. agent.

7 7.7 7

♩. = 54

General Hymns

H-197

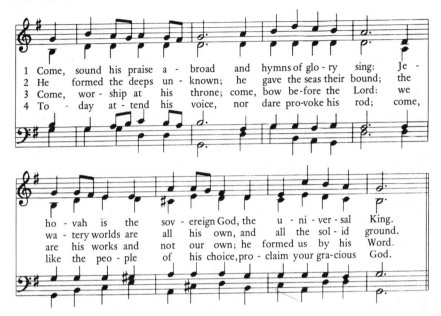

1 Come, sound his praise a - broad and hymns of glo - ry sing: Je -
2 He formed the deeps un - known; he gave the seas their bound; the
3 Come, wor - ship at his throne; come, bow be-fore the Lord: we
4 To - day at - tend his voice, nor dare pro-voke his rod; come,

ho - vah is the sov - ereign God, the u - ni - ver - sal King.
wa - tery worlds are all his own, and all the sol - id ground.
are his works and not our own; he formed us by his Word.
like the peo - ple of his choice, pro - claim your gra-cious God.

This is a metrical version of the canticle Venite, *Psalm 95.*

text: Isaac Watts, 1719.

tune: *Cambridge*, Ralph Harrison, arranged by Samuel S. Wesley.

6 6.8 6.

♩ = 58

General Hymns

H-198

1 Come, thou fount of ev - ery bless - ing, tune my
2 O to grace how great a debt - or dai - ly

heart to sing thy grace! Streams of mer - cy nev - er
I'm con - strained to be! Let thy good - ness, like a

ceas - ing, call for songs of loud - est praise. Teach me
fet - ter, bind my wan - dering heart to thee: prone to

General Hymns

some me - lo - dious son - net, sung by
wan - der, Lord, I feel it, prone to

flam - ing tongues a - bove. Praise the mount! O fix me
leave the God I love; here's my heart, O take and

on it, mount of God's un - chang - ing love.
seal it, seal it for thy courts a - bove.

text: Robert Robinson, 1758.

87.87. D

tune: *Nettleton* [Sinner's Call], American folk melody, harmonized by Alastair
Cassels-Brown, 1977. Harmony, copyright 1978 by The Church Pension Fund. ♩.= 46

H-199

text: Herbert Brokering. From *Twelve Folksongs and Spirituals*, 1968, Augsburg
Publishing House, Minneapolis, Minnesota. Used by permission.   4 5 7.D with refrain

tune: *Dexter* [Earth and All Stars], David N. Johnson, from *Twelve Folksongs
and Spirituals*, © 1968, Augsburg Publishing House. Used by permission.   ♩. = 60

H-200

1 E - ter - nal Rul - er of the cease - less round
2 We would be one in ha - tred of all wrong,
3 O clothe us with thy heaven - ly ar - mor, Lord,

of cir - cling plan-ets sing - ing on their way, guide of the
one in our love of all things sweet and fair, one with the
thy trust -y shield, thy sword of love di - vine; our in - spi -

na - tions from the night pro - found in - to the glo - ry
joy that break-eth in - to song, one with the grief that
ra - tion be thy con - stant word, we ask no vic - to -

of the per - fect day: rule in our hearts, that we may
trem - bleth in - to prayer; one in the power that makes thy
ries that are not thine; give or with - hold, let pain or

General Hymns

ev - er	be	guid - ed	and	strength-ened and	up - held by	thee.
chil - dren	free	to fol - low		truth, and thus	to fol-low	thee.
pleas-ure	be;	e - nough to		know that we	are serv-ing	thee.

text: John White Chadwick, 1864, *alt.*
tune: *Song One*, Orlando Gibbons, 1623

10 10.10 10.10 10
♩ = 52

H-201a

1 "For - give our sins as we for - give" you
2 How can your par - don reach and bless the
3 In blaz - ing light your cross re - veals the
4 Lord, cleanse the depths with - in our souls, and

taught us, Lord, to pray; but you a - lone can
un - for - giv - ing heart that broods on wrongs and
truth we dim - ly knew, how small the debts men
bid re - sent - ment cease; then, rec - on - ciled to

grant us grace to live the words we say.
will not let old bit - ter - ness de - part?
owe to us, how great our debt to you
God and man, our lives will spread your peace. A - men.

Keyboard and guitars should not be used together.

text: Rosamond Herklots. By permission of Oxford University Press.   8 6.8 6

tune: *Detroit* [Forgive our Sins], American folk melody, harmonized by Alastair
Cassels-Brown, 1977. Harmony, copyright 1978 by The Church Pension Fund. ♩ = 108

Alternate harmonization, H-201b

General Hymns

H-201b

1 "For - give our sins as we for - give"
2 How can your par - don reach and bless
3 In blaz - ing light your cross re - veals
4 Lord, cleanse the depths with - in our souls,

you taught us, Lord, to pray; but you a - lone
the un - for - giv - ing heart that broods on wrongs
the truth we dim - ly knew, how small the debts
and bid re - sent - ment cease; then, rec - on - ciled

can grant us grace to live the words we say.
and will not let old bit - ter - ness de - part?
men owe to us, how great our debt to you.
to God and man, our lives will spread your peace. A - men.

The melody is in the tenor.

text   Rosamond Herklots, By permission of Oxford University Press.

tune: *Detroit* [Forgive our Sins], American folk melody, as it appears in
       the *Southern Harmony*, (1835)

Alternate harmonization, H-201a

8 6.8 6

♩ = 108

General Hymns

H-202

Refrain:

God is love, and where true love is God him-self is there.

1 Here in Christ we gath — er, love of Christ our call — ing.
2 When we Chris-tians gath — er, mem-bers of one Bod — y,
3 Grant us love's ful-fill — ment, joy with all the bless — ed,

Christ, our love, is with us, glad-ness be his greet — ing.
let there be in us no dis-cord but one spir — it.
when we see your face, O Sav-ior, in its glo — ry.

Let us fear him, yes, and love him, God e-ter — nal.
Ban-ished now be an — ger, strife and ev-ery quar — rel.
Shine on us, O pur — est Light of all cre-a — tion,

General Hymns

Lov - ing him, let each love Christ in one an - oth - er.
Christ, our God, be al - ways pres - ent here a - mong us.
be our bliss while end - less a - ges sing your prais - es.

This is especially suitable for Maundy Thursday

text: *Ubi caritas et amor Deus ibi est*, translated by James Quinn, 1969, *alt.*
From *New Hymns for All Seasons*, copyright by Geoffrey Chapman, Ltd.
Used by permission.   13.12 12 12 12.

tune: *Ubi caritas* [God is Love] A. Gregory Murray. Copyright by A. Gregory
Murray. Used by permission of the composer.

♩ = 48

H-203

1 Glo - rious the day when Christ was born To wear the
2 Glo - rious the day when Christ a - rose, The sur - est
3 Glo - rious the days of gos - pel grace When Christ re -
4 Glo - rious the day when Christ ful - fills What man re -

crown that Cae - sars scorn, Whose life and death that
friend of all his foes; Who for the sake of
stores the fall - en race, When doubt - ers kneel and
jects yet fee - bly wills; When that strong Light puts

love re - veal Which all men need and need to feel.
those he grieves Tran - scends the world he nev - er leaves.
wave - rers stand, And faith a - chieves what rea - son planned.
out the sun And all is end - ed, all be - gun.

Refrain

Al - le - lu - ia, Al - le - lu - ia, Al - le - lu - ia!

text: F. Pratt Green, 1969. By permission of Oxford University Press.
tune: *Psalm 47*, Heinrich Schütz.

88.88 with alleluias
♩. = 40

General Hymns

H-204

1 God of mer - cy, God of grace, show the bright - ness
2 Let thy peo - ple praise thee, Lord; be by all that

of thy face. Shine up - on us, Sav - ior, shine,
live a - dored. Let the na - tions shout and sing

fill thy Church with light di - vine, and thy sav - ing
glo - ry to their Sav - ior King. Let all be, be -

health ex - tend un - to earth's re - mot - est end.
low, a - bove, one in joy, and light, and love. A - men.

text: Henry Francis Lyte, 1834, based on Psalm 67, *alt.*   77.77.77

tune: *Ratisbon*, Melody from Johann Werner's *Choral-Buch*, harmonized by Alec Wyton,
        1978. Harmony, copyright 1978 by The Church Pension Fund.
        All Rights Reserved.   ♩ = 50

Alternate harmonization, The Hymnal, No. 153

General Hymns

H-205

1 Guide me, O thou great Je-ho-vah, pil-grim through this bar-ren land;
2 O-pen now the crys-tal foun-tain, whence the heal-ing stream doth flow;
3 When I tread the verge of Jor-dan, bid my anx-ious fears sub-side;

I am weak, but thou art might-y; hold me with thy power-ful hand;
let the fire and cloud-y pil-lar lead me all my jour-ney through;
death of death, and hell's de-struc-tion, land me safe on Ca-naan's side;

bread of heav-en, bread of heav-en, feed me now and ev-er-
strong de-liv-erer, strong de-liv-erer, be thou still my strength and
songs of prais-es, songs of prais-es, I will ev-er give to

more, feed me now and ev-er-more.
shield, be thou still my strength and shield.
thee, I will ev-er give to thee. A-men.

Text: *Arglwydd arwain trwy'r anialwch*, William Williams, 1745, translated by
Peter Williams, 1772, *alt.*   8 7.8 7.8 77

tune: *Cwm Rhondda*, John Hughes, 1905 © by Mrs. Dilys Webb % Mechanical
Copyright Protection Society Limited, and reproduced by permission of the
legal representatives of the composer who reserve all rights therein.   ♩ = 46

General Hymns

H-206

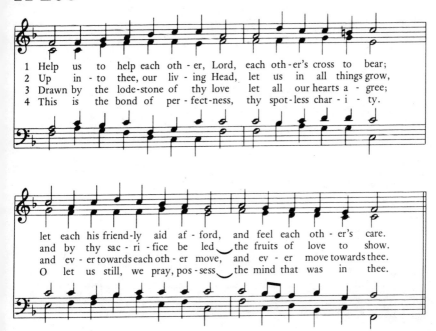

1 Help us to help each oth-er, Lord, each oth-er's cross to bear;
2 Up in-to thee, our liv-ing Head, let us in all things grow,
3 Drawn by the lode-stone of thy love let all our hearts a-gree;
4 This is the bond of per-fect-ness, thy spot-less char-i-ty.

let each his friend-ly aid af-ford, and feel each oth-er's care.
and by thy sac-ri-fice be led the fruits of love to show.
and ev-er towards each oth-er move, and ev-er move towards thee.
O let us still, we pray, pos-sess the mind that was in thee.

text: Charles Wesley, 1742, *alt.*
tune: *Dunfermline,* melody from the *Scottish Psalter* (1635)

8 6.8 6.
♩ = 46

General Hymns

H-207a

1 Ho - ly Ghost, dis - pel our sad - ness; pierce the clouds of
2 Au - thor of the new cre - a - tion, come with unc - tion

na - ture's night; come, thou source of joy and glad - ness,
and with power. Make our hearts thy hab - i - ta - tion;

breathe thy life, and spread thy light. From the height which knows no meas - ure,
with thy grace our spir - its show'r. Hear, O hear our sup - pli - ca - tion,

General Hymns

as   a   gra-cious   show'r   de - scend,   bring-ing   down   the
bless-ed   Spir-it,   God   of   peace!   Rest   up-on   this

rich-est   treas-ure   we   can   wish, or   God   can   send.
con-gre-ga-tion,   with   the   ful-ness   of   thy grace.   A - men.

text: *O du allersüsste Freude*, Paul Gerhardt, 1648, translated by
        John C. Jacobi, 1725, *alt.*   87.87.D.

tune: *Jefferson*, American folk melody, harmonized by Richard Hillert from *The Worship
        Supplement*, © 1969 by Concordia Publishing House. Used by permission.   ♩ = 50

Alternate harmonization, H-207b

Alternate tune, *Hyfrydol*, The Hymnal, No. 347².

H-207b

1 Ho - ly Ghost, dis - pel our sad - ness; pierce the clouds of na-ture's night;
2 Au - thor of the new cre - a - tion, come with unc - tion and with power.

come, thou source of joy and glad-ness, breathe thy life, and spread thy light.
Make our hearts thy hab - i - ta - tion; with thy grace our spir - its show'r.

From the height which knows no meas-ure, as a gra-cious show'r de-scend,
Hear, O hear our sup - pli - ca - tion, bless-ed Spir - it, God of peace!

bring-ing down the rich-est treas-ure we can wish, or God can send.
Rest up - on this con - gre-ga-tion, with the ful - ness of thy grace. A-men.

The melody is in the tenor.

text: *O du allersüsste Freude*, Paul Gerhardt, 1648, translated by
John C. Jacobi, 1725, *alt.*

87.87.D

tune: *Jefferson*, American folk melody, as it appears in the *Southern Harmony*, (1835) ♩ = 50

Alternate harmonization, H-207a

Alternate tune, *Hyfrydol*, The Hymnal, No. 347².

General Hymns

H-208

text: Timothy Rees, *alt.* Used by permission of A.R. Mowbray & Co. Ltd.

tune: *Abbot's Leigh*, Cyril Vincent Taylor, 1941. From the *BBC Hymn Book* by permission of Oxford University Press.

Alternate tune, *Austria*, The Hymnal, No. 385

87.87.D

♩ = 90

General Hymns

H-209a

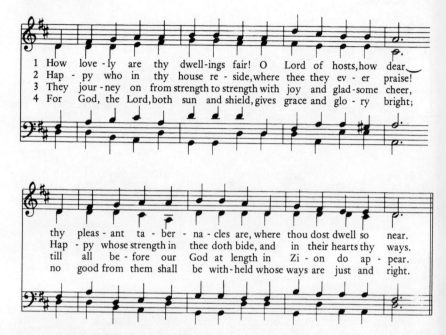

1 How love-ly are thy dwell-ings fair! O Lord of hosts, how dear
2 Hap - py who in thy house re - side, where thee they ev - er praise!
3 They jour - ney on from strength to strength with joy and glad-some cheer,
4 For God, the Lord, both sun and shield, gives grace and glo - ry bright;

thy pleas - ant ta - ber - na - cles are, where thou dost dwell so near.
Hap - py whose strength in thee doth bide, and in their hearts thy ways.
till all be - fore our God at length in Zi - on do ap - pear.
no good from them shall be with-held whose ways are just and right.

text: John Milton, 1648, *alt.* based on Psalm 84.
tune: *Tallis' Ordinal*, Thomas Tallis, ca. 1561.
Alternate harmonization with fauxbourdon, H-209b

8 6.8 6
♩ = 46

General Hymns

H-209b

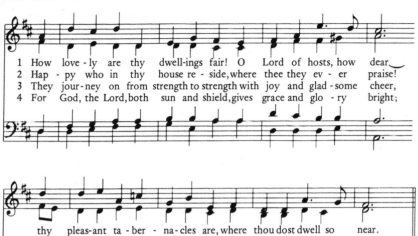

1 How love-ly are thy dwell-ings fair! O Lord of hosts, how dear
2 Hap-py who in thy house re-side, where thee they ev-er praise!
3 They jour-ney on from strength to strength with joy and glad-some cheer,
4 For God, the Lord, both sun and shield, gives grace and glo-ry bright;

thy pleas-ant ta-ber-na-cles are, where thou dost dwell so near.
Hap-py whose strength in thee doth bide, and in their hearts thy ways.
till all be-fore our God at length in Zi-on do ap-pear.
no good from them shall be with-held whose ways are just and right.

The melody is in the tenor.

text: John Milton, 1648, *alt.* based on Psalm 84.

8 6.8 6

tune: *Tallis' Ordinal*, Thomas Tallis, ca. 1561, fauxbourdon by Elizabeth
Poston. Fauxbourdon copyright 1967 by Elizabeth Poston, from *The
Cambridge Hymnal*, performing and mechanical reproduction rights
controlled by Cambridge University Press, all other rights controlled
by the composer. Used by permission.

♩ = 46

Alternate harmonization, H-209a

H-210

1 How won-drous great, how glo-rious bright must our cre-a-tor
2 Our soar-ing spir-its up-ward rise to-wards the burn-ing
3 Our rea-son stretch-es all its wings, and climbs a-bove the
4 While all the heaven-ly powers con-spire e-ter-nal praise to

be, who dwells a-midst the daz-zling light of vast e-ter-ni-ty.
throne. Fain would we see the bless-ed Three in the al-might-y One.
skies; but still how far be-neath thy feet our ground-ling know-ledge lies!
sing, let faith in hum-ble notes a-dore the great mys-te-rious King.

text: Isaac Watts, 1707, St. 3 altered by Caryl Micklem. 8.6.8.6

tune: *Shorney*, Alec Wyton, 1976. Copyright © 1977 by Agape, Carol Stream,
IL 60187. International Copyright Secured. All Rights Reserved.
Used by Permission.

♩ = 63

General Hymns

H-211

1 If thou but suf - fer God to guide thee, and hope in
2 Sing, pray, and keep his ways un - swerv-ing; so do thine

him through all thy ways, he'll give thee strength what - e'er be -
own part faith - ful - ly, and trust his word, though un - de -

tide thee, and bear thee through the e - vil days. Who trusts in
serv - ing; thou yet shalt find it true for thee; God nev - er

God's un - chang - ing love builds on a rock that nought can move.
yet for - sook at need the soul that trust - ed him in - deed.

text: *Wer nur den lieben Gott lässt walten*, Georg Neumark, 1657, translated
by Catherine Winkworth, 1863, *alt.*

98.98.88

tune: *Wer nur den lieben Gott* [Neumark], melody by Georg Neumark, 1640,
arrangement as in *More Hymns and Spiritual Songs*, © copyright 1971 by
The Walton Music Corporation. International copyright secured.
All rights reserved. Used by permission.

♩ = 108

General Hymns

H-212a

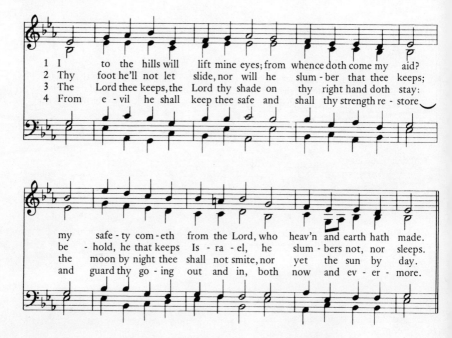

1 I to the hills will lift mine eyes; from whence doth come my aid?
2 Thy foot he'll not let slide, nor will he slum - ber that thee keeps;
3 The Lord thee keeps, the Lord thy shade on thy right hand doth stay:
4 From e - vil he shall keep thee safe and shall thy strength re - store

my safe - ty com - eth from the Lord, who heav'n and earth hath made.
be - hold, he that keeps Is - ra - el, he slum - bers not, nor sleeps.
the moon by night thee shall not smite, nor yet the sun by day.
and guard thy go - ing out and in, both now and ev - er - more.

text: Stanzas 1-3, from the *Scottish Metrical Psalter* (1650), Stanza 4 by
F. Bland Tucker, 1976, based on Psalm 121. Stanza 4 copyright 1978
by The Church Pension Fund.

8 6.8 6

tune: *Dundee*, melody from the *Scottish Psalter*, (1615).

♩ = 42

Alternate harmonization, H-212b

General Hymns

H-212b

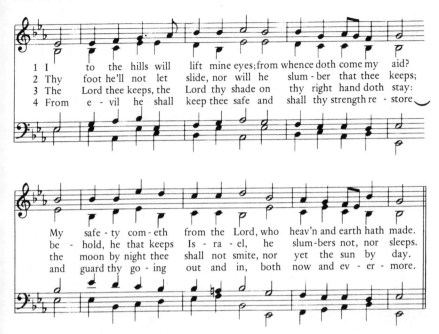

1 I to the hills will lift mine eyes; from whence doth come my aid?
2 Thy foot he'll not let slide, nor will he slum-ber that thee keeps;
3 The Lord thee keeps, the Lord thy shade on thy right hand doth stay:
4 From e-vil he shall keep thee safe and shall thy strength re-store

My safe-ty com-eth from the Lord, who heav'n and earth hath made.
be-hold, he that keeps Is-ra-el, he slum-bers not, nor sleeps.
the moon by night thee shall not smite, nor yet the sun by day.
and guard thy go-ing out and in, both now and ev-er-more.

The melody is in the tenor.

text: Stanzas 1-3, from the *Scottish Metrical Psalter* (1650), Stanza 4 by
F. Bland Tucker, 1976, based on Psalm 121. Stanza 4 copyright 1978
by The Church Pension Fund.

tune: *Dundee*, from the *Scottish Psalter* (1635).

Alternate harmonization, H212a

8 6.8 6

♩ = 42

General Hymns

H-213

Je - su, Je - su, fill us with your love, show

us how to serve the neigh-bors we have from you.

1 Kneels at the feet of his friends, si - lent - ly wash - es their
2 Neigh-bors are rich and poor, neigh-bors are black and
3 These are the ones we should serve, these are the ones we should
4 Lov - ing puts us on our knees, serv - ing as though we were

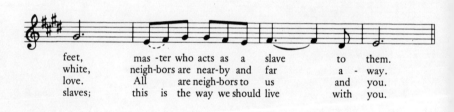

feet, mas -ter who acts as a slave to them.
white, neigh-bors are near-by and far a - way.
love. All are neigh-bors to us and you.
slaves; this is the way we should live with you.

General Hymns

text: Traditional text from Ghana, translated by Tom Colvin, *alt.*

tune: *Ghana Folk Song*, traditional Ghanian folk song.

Irr.

♩. = 72

H-214

1 Lord, be thy word my rule; in it may I re-joice;
  thy glo-ry be my aim, thy ho-ly will my choice.

2 Thy prom-is-es my hope; thy prov-i-dence my guard;
  thine arm my strong sup-port; thy-self my great re-ward.

text: Christopher Wordsworth, 1862.
tune: *Quam Dilecta*, Henry Jenner, 1861.

66.66
♩ = 52

General Hymns

H-215

1 Lord, let your ser-vant go in peace, your word is now ful-filled.
2 This is the Sav-ior of us all, the Gen-tiles' prom-ised Light,

These eyes have seen sal - va-tion's dawn, this Child so long fore-told.
God's glo - ry dwell-ing in our midst, the joy of Is - ra - el.

This is a metrical version of the canticle Nunc dimittis.

text: James Quinn, 1969, *alt.* From *New Hymns for All Seasons*, copyright
        by Geoffrey Chapman, Ltd. Used by permission.

tune: *Culross*, melody from the *Scottish Psalter* (1634)

8 6.8 6
♩ = 52

H-216

1 Lord, thou hast searched me and dost know
2 My words from thee I can-not hide;
3 Where can I go a - part from thee,
4 If I the wings of morn - ing take,
5 If deep - est dark - ness cov - er me,

1 where - e'er I rest, wher-e'er I go; thou know-est
2 I feel thy power on ev - ery side; O won-drous
3 or whith-er from thy pres - ence flee? In heaven? It
4 and far a - way my dwell - ing make, the hand that
5 the dark-ness hid - eth not from thee; to thee both

1 all that I have planned, and all my ways are in thy hand.
2 knowl-edge, aw-ful might, un - fath-omed depth, un-meas-ured height!
3 is thy dwell-ing fair; in death's a - bode? Lo, thou art there.
4 lead - eth me is thine, and my sup - port thy power di - vine.
5 night and day are bright, the dark-ness shin-eth as the light.

General Hymns

Sharps in parenthesis are to be used in the last stanza only.

text: Based on Psalm 139, from *The Psalter Hymnal* (1927)   88.88

tune: *Tender Thought*, American folk melody, harmonized by Alastair Cassels-
Brown, 1977. Harmony, copyright 1978 by The Church Pension Fund.   ♩ = 50

H-217

1 My song is love un - known, my
2 He came from his blest throne, sal -
*3 Some - times they strew his way, and
*4 Why, what hath my Lord done? What
*5 They rise, and needs will have my
6 Here might I stay and sing, no

1 Sav - ior's love to me, love to the love - less
2 va - tion to be - stow, but men made strange, and
3 his strong prais - es sing, re - sound - ing all the
4 makes this rage and spite? He made the lame to
5 dear Lord made a - way; a mur - der - er they
6 sto - ry so di - vine: nev - er was love, dear

1 shown that they might love - ly be. O
2 none the longed - for Christ would know. But
3 day ho - san - nas to their King. Then
4 run, he gave the blind their sight. Sweet
5 save, the Prince of Life they slay. Yet
6 King, nev - er was grief like thine. This

General Hymns

```
1 who    am    I        that   for    my     sake      my
2 O      my    friend,  my     friend in  -  deed,     who
3 "Cru - ci - fy"       is     all    their breath,    and
4 in - ju - ries!       yet    they   at    these      them -
5 cheer - ful he        to     suf - f'ring goes,      that
6 is     my    friend,  in     whose  sweet praise      I
```

```
1 Lord   should take    frail  flesh,  and    die.
2 at     my     need    his    life    did    spend.
3 for    his    death   they   thirst  and    cry.
4 selves dis -  please, and    'gainst him    rise.
5 he     his    foes    from   thence  might  free.
6 all    my     days    could  glad - ly      spend.
```

Stanzas 3, 4, 5 may be omitted.

text: Samuel Crossman, ca. 1664.

tune: *Love Unknown*, John Ireland, 1925. This tune is copyright and is
printed here by permission of the owner, Mrs. Norah Kirby.

66.66.44.44

♩ = 50

H-218a

1 My shep - herd will sup - ply my need; Je -
2 When I walk through the shades of death, thy
3 The sure pro - vi - sions of my God at -

ho - vah is his Name; in pas - tures fresh he
pres - ence is my stay; one word of thy sup -
tend me all my days; O may thy house be

makes me feed, be - side the liv - ing stream. He
port - ing breath drives all my fears a - way. Thy
my a - bode and all my work be praise. There

General Hymns

brings my wan - d'ring spir - it back when I for -
hand, in sight of all my foes, doth still my
would I find . a set - tled rest, while oth - ers

sake his ways, and leads me for his
ta - ble spread; my cup with bless - ings
go and come; no more a stran - ger

mer - cy's sake in paths of truth and grace.
o - ver - flows, thy oil a - noints my head.
or a guest, but like a child at home.

This is a metrical paraphrase of Psalm 23.

text: Isaac Watts, 1719.

8.6.8.6

tune: *Resignation,* American folk melody, harmonized by David Hurd, 1978.
Harmony, copyright 1978 by The Church Pension Fund.

♩. = 42

Alternate harmonization, H-218b

H-218b

1 My shep-herd will sup-ply my need; Je-ho-vah is his Name;
2 When I walk through the shades of death, thy pres-ence is my stay;
3 The sure pro-vi-sions of my God at-tend me all my days;

in pas-tures fresh he makes me feed, be-side the liv-ing stream.
one word of thy sup-port-ing breath drives all my fears a-way.
O may thy house be my a-bode and all my work be praise.

He brings my wan-d'ring spir-it back when I for-sake his ways,
Thy hand, in sight of all my foes, doth still my ta-ble spread;
There would I find a set-tled rest, while oth-ers go and come;

and leads me for his mer-cy's sake in paths of truth and grace.
my cup with bless-ings o-ver-flows, thy oil a-noints my head.
no more a stran-ger or a guest, but like a child at home.

General Hymns

The melody is in the tenor.

This is a metrical paraphrase of Psalm 23.

text: Isaac Watts, 1719.

tune: *Resignation,* American folk melody, as it appears in the
        Southern Harmony (1835).

Alternate harmonization, H-218a

8.6.8.6

♩. = 42

H-219

1 Na - ture with o - pen vol - ume stands to spread her
2 But in the grace that res - cued man, his bright - est
3 Here his whole Name ap - pears com - plete; nor wit can
4 O the sweet won - ders of that cross where Christ my
5 I would for - ev - er speak his name in sounds to

1 Mak - er's praise a - broad; and ev' - ry la - bor of his
2 form of glo - ry shines; here, on the cross, 'tis fair - est
3 guess, nor rea - son prove, which of the let - ters best is
4 Sav - ior loved and died! Her no - blest life my spir - it
5 mor - tal ears un - known, with an - gels join to praise the

1 hands shows some - thing wor - thy of a God.
2 drawn in pre - cious blood and crim - son lines.
3 writ, the power, the wis - dom, or the love.
4 draws from his dear wounds and bleed - ing side.
5 Lamb and wor - ship at his Fa - ther's throne!

General Hymns

text: Isaac Watts, 1707.

tune: *Eltham*, melody by Nathaniel Hawthorne, harmonized by Samuel Sebastian
        Wesley and edited by Erik Routley. Copyright 1977 by Agape, Carol Stream,
        IL 60187. International Copyright Secured. All Rights Reserved.
        Used by Permission.

8 8.8 8.

♩ = 52

H-220

1 New songs of cel - e - bra - tion ren - der
2 Joy - ful - ly, heart - i - ly re - sound - ing,
3 Riv - ers and seas and tor - rents roar - ing,

to him who has great won - ders done;
let ev - ery in - stru - ment and voice
hon - or the Lord with wild ac - claim;

awed by his power his foes sur - ren - der
peal out the praise of grace a - bound - ing,
moun - tains and stones look up a - dor - ing,

and fall be - fore the might - y One.
call - ing the whole world to re - joice.
and find a voice to praise his Name.

General Hymns

He has made known his great sal - va - tion
Trum - pets and or - gans set in mo - tion
Right - eous, com - mand - ing, ev - er glo - rious,

which all his friends with joy con - fess;
such sounds as make the heav - ens ring:
prais - es be his that nev - er cease:

he has re - vealed to eve - ry na - tion
all things that live in earth and o - cean
just - is our God, whose truth vic - to - rious

his ev - er - last - ing right - eous - ness.
make mu - sic for your might - y King.
es - tab - lish - es the world in peace.

This is a metrical version of Psalm 98.

text: Erik Routley. Copyright © 1974 by Agape, Carol Stream, IL 60187.
        International Copyright Secured. All Rights Reserved.
        Used by Permission.   78.98.D.

tune: *Rendez à Dieu*, Louis Bourgeois, 1543, adapted by Erik Routley.
        Adaptation Copyright 1974 by Agape, Carol Stream, IL 60187.
        International Copyright Secured. All Rights Reserved. Used by Permission.   ♩ = 48

Alternative harmonization, The Hymnal, No. 195.

H-221

This is a metrical version of the canticle Benedicite, omnia opera Domini

text: F. Bland Tucker, 1978. Copyright 1978 by The Church Pension Fund.   8 6.8 6

tune: *Montrose*, from Gilmour's *Psalm-Singer's Assistant* (1793), harmonization
by Erik Routley, 1976. From *Westminster Praise* edited by Erik Routley.
Harmonization copyright 1976 by Hinshaw Music, Inc., Chapel Hill,
NC 27514. Used by permission.   ♩ = 92

Alternate tune, *Miles' Lane*, The Hymnal, No. 355²

Harmonization in a lower key, H-239

General Hymns

H-222

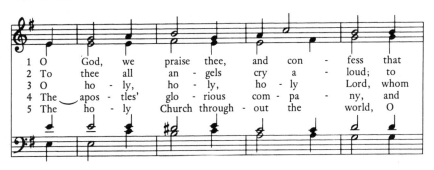

1 O God, we praise thee, and con - fess that
2 To thee all an - gels cry a - loud; to
3 O ho - ly, ho - ly, ho - ly Lord, whom
4 The apos - tles' glo - rious com - pa - ny, and
5 The ho - ly Church through - out the world, O

1 thou the on - ly Lord and ev - er - last - ing
2 thee the powers on high, both cher - u - bim and
3 heaven - ly hosts o - bey, the world is with the
4 proph - ets crowned with light, with all the mar - tyrs'
5 Lord, con - fess - es thee, that thou e - ter - nal

Fa - ther art, by all the earth a - dored.
ser - a - phim, con - tin - ual - ly do cry:
glo - ry filled of thy maj - es - tic sway!
no - ble host, thy con - stant praise re - cite.
Fa - ther art, of bound - less maj - es - ty.

The G-sharp may be reserved for the last stanza.

This is a metrical version of the canticle Te Deum.

text: From *A Supplement to the New Version* (1702) by Nahum Tate and
Nicholas Brady, *alt.*   8 6.8 6.

tune: *Ely,* Melody by Thomas Ravenscroft, 1621, last line altered by
John Playford, 1677. Harmonized by Russell Schulz-Widmar, 1978.
Harmony copyright 1978 by The Church Pension Fund. $\quad$. = 42

General Hymns

H-223a

1 O Ho - ly Spir - it, Lord of grace, e - ter - nal fount of love,
2 As thou in bond of love dost join the Fa - ther and the Son,

in - flame, we pray, our in - most hearts with fire from heav'n a - bove.
so fill us all with mu - tual love, u - nite our hearts as one. A - men.

text: *O fons amoris, Spiritus*, Charles Coffin, 1736, translated by
        John Chandler, 1737, *alt*.

tune: *Wigtown*, melody from the *Scottish Psalter* (1635).

Alternate harmonization, H-223b

Alternate tune, *St. Magnus* H-172

8 6.8 6.
♩ = 54

General Hymns

H-223b

1 O Ho - ly Spir - it, Lord of grace, e - ter - nal fount of love;
2 As thou in bond of love dost join the Fa - ther and the Son,

in - flame, we pray, our in - most hearts with fire from heav'n a - bove.
so fill us all with mu - tual love, u - nite our hearts as one. A - men.

The melody is in the tenor.

text: *O fons amoris, Spiritus*, Charles Coffin, 1736, translated by
        John Chandler, 1737, *alt.*

tune: *Wigtown*, melody from the *Scottish Psalter* (1635).

Alternate harmonization, H-223a

Alternate tune, *St. Magnus* H-172

8 6.8 6.
♩ = 54

H-224

1 O love of God, how strong and true,
   love,
   came
   save

e - ter - nal and yet ev - er new;
we read thee in the sky a - bove;
to bear for us the cross of shame,
e'en in the dark - ness of the grave;

un - com - pre - hend - ed and un - bought,
we read thee in the earth be - low,
sent by the Fa - ther from on high,
still more in res - ur - rec - tion light

General Hymns

be - yond all knowl - edge and all thought.
in seas that swell and streams that flow.
our life to live, our death to die.
we read the full - ness of thy might,

After stanzas 1-3   *After stanza 4*

2 O wide em - brac-ing, won-drous
3 We read thee best in him who
4 We read thy power to bless and

A - men.

The obbligato which appears in the right hand of the organ part may be sung by the sopranos, or played on a solo instrument.

text: Horatius Bonar, 1861.   88.88

tune: *De Tar*, Calvin Hampton. From Three Hymn Tunes by Calvin Hampton, © 1973
by Concordia Publishing House. Used by permission.   ♩ = 60

Alternate tune, H-225

H-225

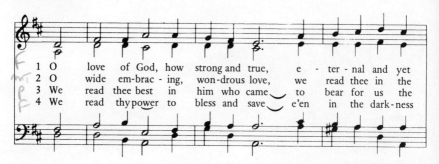

1 O love of God, how strong and true, e - ter - nal and yet
2 O wide em-brac - ing, won-drous love, we read thee in the
3 We read thee best in him who came to bear for us the
4 We read thy power to bless and save e'en in the dark-ness

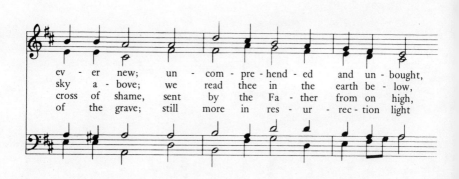

ev - er new; un - com - pre - hend - ed and un - bought,
sky a - bove; we read thee in the earth be - low,
cross of shame, sent by the Fa - ther from on high,
of the grave; still more in res - ur - rec - tion light

be - yond all knowl-edge and all thought.
in seas that swell and streams that flow.
our life to live, our death to die.
we read the full - ness of thy might. A - men.

text: Horatius Bonar, 1861.

tune: *Mach's mit mir*, *Gott* [Eisenach], Johann Hermann Schein, 1629.

Alternate tune, H-224

88.88

♩. = 42

H-226

1. O Spir-it of Life, O Spir-it of God, in ev-'ry need thou bring-est aid; thou com-est forth from God's great throne, from God, the Fa-ther and the Son; O Spir-it of Life, O Spir-it of God.

2. O Spir-it of Life, O Spir-it of God, in-crease our faith in our dear Lord; un-less thy grace the power should give, none can be-lieve in Christ and live; O Spir-it of Life, O Spir-it of God.

*3. O Spir-it of Life, O Spir-it of God, make us to love thy sa-cred Word; the ho-ly flame of love im-part, that char-i-ty may warm each heart; O Spir-it of Life, O Spir-it of God.

4. O Spir-it of Life, O Spir-it of God, en-light-en us by that same Word; teach us to know the Fa-ther's love, and his dear Son, who reigns a-bove; O Spir-it of Life, O Spir-it of God. A-men.

General Hymns

text: *O Heiliger Geist, O heiliger Gott,* Johann Niedling, 1651, translated
       by John Caspar Mattes, 1813, *alt.* From the *Lutheran Service Book and
       Hymnal,* by permission of the Commission on the Liturgy and Hymnal.   10 8.88.10

tune: *O Heiliger Geist, O heiliger Gott* [O Jesülein suss], melody from
       the *Geistliche Kirchengesang,* Köln (1623), harmonized by Johann Sebastian
       Bach, harmonization simplified by Alastair Cassels-Brown, 1977. Harmony
       adaptation copyright 1978 by The Church Pension Fund.   ♩ = 90

H-227

1 Out of the depths I cry to thee; Lord, hear me, I im - plore thee!
2 Our par - don is thy gift, thy love and grace a - lone a - vail us;
3*And though it tar - ry till the night, and round till morn - ing wak - en,
4 Though great our sins and sore our woes, his grace much more a - bound - eth;

Bend down thy gra - cious ear to me; let my prayer come be - fore thee!
our works could ne'er our guilt re - move, the strict-est life must fail us,
my heart shall ne'er mis - trust his might, nor count it - self for - sak - en.
his help - ing love no lim - it knows, our ut - most need it sound - eth;

If thou re - mem - berest each mis - deed, if each should
that none may boast them - selves of aught, but own in
Do thus, O ye of Is - rael's seed, ye of the
our kind and faith - ful shep - herd, he, who shall at

General Hymns

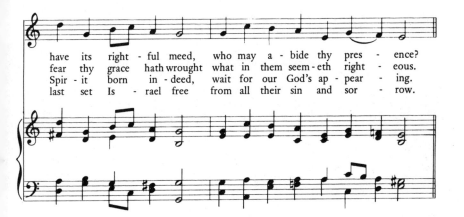

have its right - ful meed, who may a - bide thy pres - ence?
fear thy grace hath wrought what in them seem - eth right - eous.
Spir - it born in - deed, wait for our God's ap - pear - ing.
last set Is - rael free from all their sin and sor - row.

This is a metrical version of Psalm 130

text: *Aus tiefer Not schrei' ich zu dir*, Martin Luther, 1523, translated
     by Catherine Winkworth, 1863, *alt.*

tune: *Aus tiefer Not*, melody attributed to Martin Luther, 1524, harmonized
     by Austin C. Lovelace. Harmony copyright 1964 by Abingdon Press.
     Used by permission.

87.87.88 7

♩ = 44

H-228

1 Praise the Lord! ye heavens adore him; praise him, angels, in the height;
2 Praise the Lord! for he is glorious; never shall his promise fail;

sun and moon, rejoice before him; praise him, all ye stars of light.
God hath made his saints victorious; sin and death shall not prevail.

Praise the Lord! for he hath spoken; worlds his mighty voice obeyed;
Praise the God of our salvation! Hosts on high, his power proclaim;

laws which never shall be broken for their guidance hath he made.
heaven and earth, and all creation, laud and magnify his Name.

This is a metrical version of Psalm 148

text: Anonymous, from John Kempthorne's Foundling Hospital *Psalms and Hymns*, 1796.

tune: *Austria*, Franz Joseph Haydn, 1797.

87.87.D.
♩ = 46

General Hymns

H-229

1 Praise we now the word of grace; may our minds its truth em - brace;
2 May the gos - pel of the Lord ev - ery - where be spread a - broad,

from its pag - es may we hear Christ our teach - er, speak-ing clear.
that the world a - round be shown Christ as king, and Christ a - lone.

text: Sidney Newman Sedgwick.
tune: *Da Christus geboren war*, Johann Friedrich Doles.

77.77
♩ = 52

H-230

INTERLUDE BETWEEN 3 AND 4.

Optional Introduction

1 Re - joice, the Lord is King! your Lord and King a - dore!
2 The Lord the Sav - ior reigns, the God of truth and love;
3 His king-dom can - not fail; he rules o'er earth and heav'n;
4 Re - joice in glo - rious hope! Our Lord the Judge shall come,

Mor - tals, give thanks and sing, and tri - umph ev - er - more.
when he had purged our stains he took his seat a - bove.
the keys of death and hell to Christ the Lord are giv'n.
and take his ser - vants up to their e - ter - nal home.

(small notes optional)

General Hymns

ALL

Verses 1-3

Lift up your heart! lift up your voice! Re-joice! a-gain I say, re-joice!

Verse 4

Lift up your heart! lift up your voice! Re-joice! a-gain I say, re-joice!

text: Charles Wesley, 1746, *alt.*

tune: *Gopsal*, George Frederick Handel, arranged by John Wilson.
        Copyright by Oxford University Press. Used by Permission.

Alternate tune, *Darwall's 148th*, H-243

66.66.88

♩ = 112

H-231

1 Sing, all cre - a - tion, sing to God in
2 Know that our God is Lord of all the
3 En - ter his tem - ple, ring - ing out his
4 Great in his good - ness is the Lord we

glad - ness! Joy - ous - ly serve him, sing - ing hymns of
a - ges! He is our Mak - er; we are all his
prais - es! Sing in thanks - giv - ing as you come be -
wor - ship! Stead - fast his kind - ness, love that knows no

hom - age! Chant - ing his prais - es, come be - fore his
crea - tures, peo - ple he fash - ioned, sheep he leads to
fore him! Bless - ing his boun - ty, glo - ri - fy his
end - ing! Faith - ful his word is, change - less, ev - er -

General Hymns

pres	-	ence!	Praise	the	Al	-	might	-	y!
pas	-	ture!	Praise	the	Al	-	might	-	y!
great	-	ness!	Praise	the	Al	-	might	-	y!
last	-	ing!	Praise	the	Al	-	might	-	y!

This is a metrical version of the canticle Jubilate, Psalm 100

text: James Quinn, 1969. From *New Hymns for All Seasons*, copyright by
     Geoffrey Chapman, Ltd. Used by permission.

tune: *Iste Confessor* [Rouen], melody from *Rouen, Antiphonary* (1728).

Alternate harmonization, The Hymnal No. 228.

11 11.11 5

♩ = 56

H-232

1 Sing now with joy unto the Lord, for
2 God is our strength, he is our song, he
3 He only is the might-y Lord. He

he has tri-umphed glo-rious-ly! The horse, the char-iot,
saved us from our en-e-my. All praise and thanks to
on-ly can de-stroy the foe. He on-ly is to

and the sword he cast in-to the rag-ing sea.
him be-long who came to set his peo-ple free.
be a-dored for he a-lone can make us whole.

General Hymns

This is a metrical version of The Song of Miriam
text: author unknown, ca. 1976.
tune: *Tallis' Canon*, Thomas Tallis, ca. 1567.

8 8.8 8.
♩ = 46

H-233

1 Sing praise to God who reigns a-bove, the God of all cre-
2 What God's al-might-y power hath made, his gra-cious mer - cy
3 O ye who name Christ's ho - ly Name, give God all praise and

a - tion, the God of power,the God of love, the God of our
keep - eth; by morn-ing glow or eve-ning shade his watch-ful eye
glo - ry; all ye who know his power,pro-claim a - loud the won -

sal - va - tion; with heal-ing balm my soul he fills, and
ne'er sleep - eth. With - in the king-dom of his might, lo!
drous sto - ry! Cast each false i - dol from its throne,the

General Hymns

ev - ery faith-less mur-mur stills: to God all praise and glo - ry.
all is just and all is right: to God all praise and glo - ry.
Lord is God, and he a-lone: to God all praise and glo - ry.

text: *Sei Lob und Ehr dem höchsten Gut*, Johann Jakob Schütz, 1675,
translated by Frances Elizabeth Cox, 1864, *alt.*   87.87.88 7

tune: *Mit Freuden zart* [Bohemian Brethren], melody from *Krichengesang*
darinnen die Heubtartickel die Christlichen Glaubens (1566)   ♩ = 58

H-234

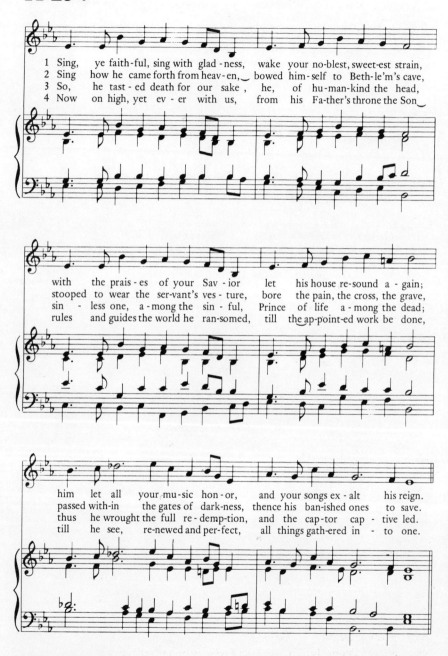

1 Sing, ye faith-ful, sing with glad-ness, wake your no-blest, sweet-est strain,
2 Sing how he came forth from heav-en, bowed him-self to Beth-le'm's cave,
3 So, he tast-ed death for our sake, he, of hu-man-kind the head,
4 Now on high, yet ev-er with us, from his Fa-ther's throne the Son

with the prais-es of your Sav-ior let his house re-sound a-gain;
stooped to wear the ser-vant's ves-ture, bore the pain, the cross, the grave,
sin-less one, a-mong the sin-ful, Prince of life a-mong the dead;
rules and guides the world he ran-somed, till the ap-point-ed work be done,

him let all your mu-sic hon-or, and your songs ex-alt his reign.
passed with-in the gates of dark-ness, thence his ban-ished ones to save.
thus he wrought the full re-demp-tion, and the cap-tor cap-tive led.
till he see, re-newed and per-fect, all things gath-ered in-to one.

General Hymns

text: John Ellerton, *alt.*

tune: *Finnian*, Christopher Dearnley, from *English Praise* by permission of
       Oxford University Press.

87.87.87

♩ = 50

H-235

1 Tell out, my soul, the great-ness of the Lord! Un-num-bered
2 Tell out, my soul, the great-ness of his Name! Make known his
3 Tell out, my soul, the great-ness of his might! Pow'rs and do—
4 Tell out, my soul, the glo-ries of his word! Firm is his

bless-ings give my spir-it voice; ten-der to me the prom-ise
might, the deeds his arm has done; his mer-cy sure, from age to
min-ions lay their glo-ry by; proud hearts and stub-born wills are
prom-ise, and his mer-cy sure. Tell out, my soul, the great-ness

of his word; in God my Sav-ior shall my heart re-joice.
age the same; his ho-ly Name—the Lord, the might-y One.
put to flight, the hun-gry fed, the hum-ble lift-ed high.
of the Lord to chil-dren's chil-dren and for-ev-er-more!

This is a metrical version of the canticle Magnificat

text: Timothy Dudley-Smith. By permission of the author.   10 10.10 10

tune: *Birmingham*, from Francis Cunningham's *A Selection of Psalm Tunes* (1834)   ♩ = 54

General Hymns

H-236

1 The gates of death are bro-ken through, the strength of hell is tamed,
2 A clear-er light now spreads its ray a-cross the land of gloom
3 For so the true cre-a-tor died that sin-ners might not die,

and by the ho-ly cross a-new its cru-el king is shamed.
since he who made the pri-mal day re-stores it from the tomb.
and so he has been cru-ci-fied that we might rise on high.

text: *Mortis portis fractis fortis*, Peter of St. Maurice, ca. 1115   8 6.8 6.

tune: *Venerable*, Vincent Persichetti. From *Hymns and Responses for the
       Church Year* by Vincent Persichetti. © 1956 by Elkan-Vogal, Inc.
       Used by permission.   ♩ = 56

Alternate tune, *Bangor*, The Hymnal, No. 68

General Hymns

H-237

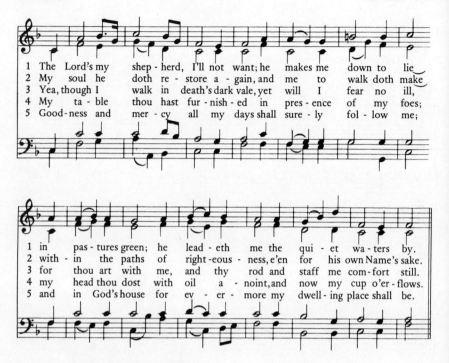

1 The Lord's my shep-herd, I'll not want; he makes me down to lie
2 My soul he doth re-store a-gain, and me to walk doth make
3 Yea, though I walk in death's dark vale, yet will I fear no ill,
4 My ta-ble thou hast fur-nish-ed in pres-ence of my foes;
5 Good-ness and mer-cy all my days shall sure-ly fol-low me;

1 in pas-tures green; he lead-eth me the qui-et wa-ters by.
2 with-in the paths of right-eous-ness, e'en for his own Name's sake.
3 for thou art with me, and thy rod and staff me com-fort still.
4 my head thou dost with oil a-noint, and now my cup o'er-flows.
5 and in God's house for ev-er-more my dwell-ing place shall be.

This is a metrical version of Psalm 23.

text: from *The Scottish Psalter* (1650), *alt.*

tune: *Crimond*, melody by Jessie Seymour Irvine.

8 6.8 6.

♩ = 90

General Hymns

H-238

1 The water stood like walls of brass, to
let the tribes of Is-rael pass; and from the rock in
riv-ers burst, at Mo-ses' prayer to quench their thirst.

General Hymns

Optional descant (verse 3 or 4)

2 The fire re-strained by God's com-mands could on-ly burn his
3 Thus crea-tures on-ly can ful-fill their great cre-a-tor's
4 Then let us trust the Lord a-lone, and crea-ture-con-fi-

peo-ple's bands; too faint, when he was with them there, to
ho-ly will; and when his ser-vants need their aid, his
dence dis-own; nor if they threat-en need we fear, they

singe their gar-ments or their hair. At Da-niel's feet the
pur-pos-es must be o-beyed. So if his bless-ing
can-not hurt if he be near. If in-stru-ments of

li - ons lay like harm-less lambs, nor touched their prey; and
he re - fuse, their pow'r to help they quick - ly lose, sure
pain they prove, still are they guid - ed by his love; as

ra - vens,which on car-rion fed, pro - cured E - li -jah flesh and bread.
as on crea-tures we de - pend,our hopes in dis-ap - point-ment end.
lan-cets by the sur-geon's skill,which wound to cure,and not to kill.

Fine

text: John Newton, 1779, *alt.*   88.88

tune: *St. Olaf's*, John Gardner. © John Gardner, all rights controlled by
       Cambridge University Press. Used by permission.   ♩ = 100

Alternate tune, *Breslau*, The Hymnal, No. 6²

H-239

1 The Lord will come and not be slow, his foot-steps can-not err;
2 Truth from the earth, like to a flower, shall bud and blos-som then;
3 Rise, God, judge thou the earth in might, this wick-ed earth re - dress;
4 The na - tions all whom thou hast made shall come, and all shall frame
5 For great thou art, and won-ders great by thy strong hand are done;

1 be - fore him right-eous-ness shall go, his roy - al har - bin - ger.
2 and jus - tice, from her heav'n-ly bower, look down on mor - tal men.
3 for thou art he who shalt by right the na - tions all pos - sess.
4 to bow them low be - fore thee, Lord, and glo - ri - fy thy Name.
5 thou in thy ev - er - last - ing seat re - main - est God a - lone.

text: John Milton, 1648, based on Psalms 82, 85, and 86. 8 6.8 6

tune: *Montrose*, from Gilmour's *Psalm-Singer's Assistant* (1793) harmonized
by Erik Routley, 1976. From *Westminster Praise* edited by Erik Routley.
Harmonization copyright © 1976 by Hinshaw Music, Inc., Chapel Hill,
NC 27514. Used by permission. ♩ = 92

This setting is available in a higher key at H-221
Alternate tunes, *York* and *Balfour*, The Hymnal, No. 312¹, 312²

General Hymns

H-240

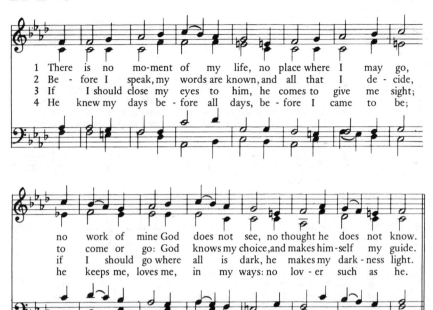

1 There is no mo-ment of my life, no place where I may go,
2 Be - fore I speak, my words are known, and all that I de - cide,
3 If I should close my eyes to him, he comes to give me sight;
4 He knew my days be - fore all days, be - fore I came to be;

no work of mine God does not see, no thought he does not know.
to come or go: God knows my choice, and makes him-self my guide.
if I should go where all is dark, he makes my dark - ness light.
he keeps me, loves me, in my ways: no lov - er such as he.

This is a metrical version of Psalm 139.

text: Brian Foley. From the *New Catholic Hymnal*. Reprinted by Permission
of Faber Music. Ltd.
tune: *Burford*, from John Chetham's *Book of Psalmody* (1718).

8 6.8 6
♩ = 102

General Hymns

H-241

1 This is my Fa-ther's world, and to my lis-tening ears
2 This is my Fa-ther's world, the birds their car-ols raise,
3 This is my Fa-ther's world, O let us not for - get

all na-ture sings, and round me rings the mu -sic of the spheres.
the morn-ing light, the li - ly white, de - clare their Mak-er's praise.
that though the wrong is great and strong, God is our Fa - ther yet.

This is my Fa-ther's world: I rest me in the thought of
This is my Fa-ther's world: he shines in all that's fair; in the
He trusts us with his world, to keep it clean and fair, all

rocks and trees, of skies and seas his hand the won-ders wrought.
rust - ling grass I hear him pass, he speaks to me ev - ery - where.
earth and trees, all skies and seas, all crea - tures ev - ery - where.

General Hymns

text: Maltbie D. Babcock, 1901, Stanza 3 altered by Mary Babcock Crawford, 1972. Used by permission of Mary Babcock Crawford.　　　　6 6.8 6.D.

tune: *Mercer Street*, Malcolm Williamson. Copyright © 1975 by Agape. International Copyright Secured. All Rights Reserved. Used by Permission.　　♩ = 72

H-242

Guitars or keyboard may be used separately or together.

text: Anonymous Shaker song.

tune: *Simple Gifts*, anonymous Shaker melody, harmonized by Alastair Cassels-Brown, 1977. Harmony, copyright 1978 by The Church Pension Fund. All Rights Reserved.

Irr.

♩ = 116

H-243

1 To God with glad - ness sing, your Rock and Sav - ior
2 He cra - dles in his hand the heights and depths of
3 Your heav'n - ly Fa - ther praise, ac - claim his on - ly

bless; with - in his tem - ple bring your songs of
earth; he made the sea and land, he brought the
Son, your voice in hom - age raise to him who

thank - ful - ness! O God of might, to
world to birth! O God most high, we
makes all one! O Dove of peace, on

you we sing, en - throned as King on heav - en's height!
are your sheep; on us you keep your shep - herd's eye!
us de - scend that strife may end and joy in - crease!

General Hymns

This is a metrical version of the canticle Venite, Psalm 95.

text: James Quinn, 1969. From *New Hymns for All Seasons*, copyright by
        Geoffrey Chapman, Ltd. Used by permission.   66.66.44.44

tune: *Darwall's 148th*, John Darwall, 1770.   ♩ = 58

H-244

1. What does the Lord re - quire for praise and of - fer - ing?
2. Ru - lers of earth, give ear! should you not jus - tice show?
3. How shall our life ful - fill God's law so hard and high?

What sac - ri - fice, de - sire or tri - bute bid you
Will God your plead - ing hear, while crime and cru - el - ty
Let Christ en - due our will with grace to for - ti -

bring? Do just - ly; love mer - cy; walk
grow? Do just - ly; love mer - cy; walk
fy. Then just - ly, in mer - cy we'll

General Hymns

hum - bly with your God.
hum - bly with your God.

hum - bly walk with God.

text: Alfred F. Bayly, abridged and altered. Text copyright. Used by permission of the author.

tune: *Sharpthorne*, Erik Routley. Music Copyright. Used by permission of the composer.

66.66.33.6

♩ = 50

H-245a

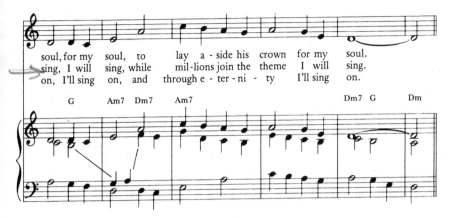

soul, for my soul, to lay a - side his crown for my soul.
sing, I will sing, while mil-lions join the theme I will sing.
on, I'll sing on, and through e - ter - ni - ty I'll sing on.

Guitars and keyboard may sound together for good effect.

The bass-line may be sung in canon with the soprano.

text: American folk hymn, attributed to Alex Means, ca. 1835.

tune: *Wondrous Love*, American folk melody, harmonized by Alastair Cassels-Brown, 1977. Harmony, copyright 1978 by The Church Pension Fund.

Alternate harmonization, H-245b

12 9.12 12 9

♩ = 60

H-245b

1 What won-drous love is this, O my soul, O my soul, what
2 To God and to the Lamb, I will sing, I will sing, to
3 And when from death I'm free, I'll sing on, I'll sing on, and

won-drous love is this, O my soul. What won-drous love is this that
God and to the Lamb, I will sing. To God and to the Lamb who
when from death I'm free, I'll sing on. And when from death I'm free, I'll

caused the Lord of bliss to lay a - side his crown for my
is the great I AM, while mil - lions join the theme I will
sing and joy - ful be, and through e - ter - ni - ty I'll sing

soul, for my soul, to lay a - side his crown for my soul.
sing, I will sing, while mil - lions join the theme I will sing.
on, I'll sing on, and through e - ter - ni - ty I'll sing on.

General Hymns

The melody is in the tenor.

text: American folk hymn, attributed to Alex Means, ca. 1835.

tune: *Wondrous Love,* American folk hymn, as found in
        The Southern Harmony (1835)

Alternate harmonization, H-245a

12 9.12 12 9

♩ = 60

H-246

1 Where is this stu-pen-dous stran-ger? Proph-ets, shep-herds, kings, ad-vise,
2 O most might-y, O most ho-ly, far be-yond the ser-aph's thought
3 O the mag-ni-tude of meek-ness! Worth from worth im-mor-tal sprung,
4 God all-boun-teous, all-cre-a-tive, whom no ills from good dis-suade,

lead me to my Mas-ter's man-ger, show me where my Sav-ior lies.
art thou then so mean and low-ly as un-heed-ed proph-ets taught?
O the strength of in-fant weak-ness, if e-ter-nal is so young!
is in-car-nate and a na-tive of the ver-y world he made.

The fermata is suggested for the last stanza only.

text: Christopher Smart, 1765. *alt.*

tune: *Kit Smart*, Alec Wyton, 1976. Copyright © 1976 by Agape, Carol Stream, IL 60187, International Copyright Secured. All Rights Reserved. Used by Permission.

87.87

♩ = 72

H-247a

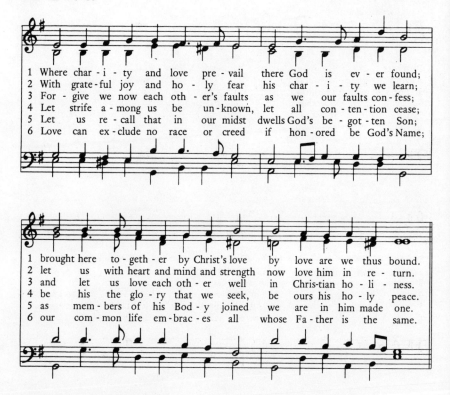

1 Where char-i-ty and love pre-vail there God is ev-er found;
2 With grate-ful joy and ho-ly fear his char-i-ty we learn;
3 For-give we now each oth-er's faults as we our faults con-fess;
4 Let strife a-mong us be un-known, let all con-ten-tion cease;
5 Let us re-call that in our midst dwells God's be-got-ten Son;
6 Love can ex-clude no race or creed if hon-ored be God's Name;

1 brought here to-geth-er by Christ's love by love are we thus bound.
2 let us with heart and mind and strength now love him in re-turn.
3 and let us love each oth-er well in Chris-tian ho-li-ness.
4 be his the glo-ry that we seek, be ours his ho-ly peace.
5 as mem-bers of his Bod-y joined we are in him made one.
6 our com-mon life em-brac-es all whose Fa-ther is the same.

This is especially suitable for Maundy Thursday.

text: *Ubi caritas et amor Deus ibi est.* Translated by J. Clifford Evers, 1961.
English translation. © 1975 by G.I.A. Publications, Inc.,
from Worship II. Used by permission.

8 6.8 6.
♩ = 54

tune: *Cheshire*, melody from Este's *Psalter* (1592), rhythm slightly altered.
Alternate harmonization, H-246b

General Hymns

H-247b

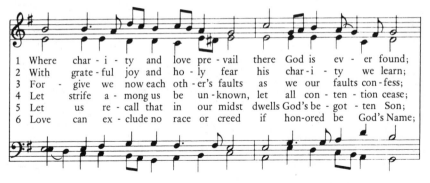

1 Where char - i - ty and love pre - vail there God is ev - er found;
2 With grate - ful joy and ho - ly fear his char - i - ty we learn;
3 For - give we now each oth - er's faults as we our faults con - fess;
4 Let strife a - mong us be un - known, let all con - ten - tion cease;
5 Let us re - call that in our midst dwells God's be - got - ten Son;
6 Love can ex - clude no race or creed if hon - ored be God's Name;

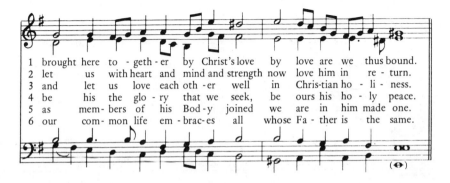

1 brought here to - geth - er by Christ's love by love are we thus bound.
2 let us with heart and mind and strength now love him in re - turn.
3 and let us love each oth - er well in Chris-tian ho - li - ness.
4 be his the glo - ry that we seek, be ours his ho - ly peace.
5 as mem - bers of his Bod - y joined we are in him made one.
6 our com - mon life em - brac - es all whose Fa - ther is the same.

The melody is in the tenor.

This is especially suitable for Maundy Thursday.

text: *Ubi caritas et amor Deus ibi est*, translated by J. Clifford Evers, 1961.
        English translation © 1975 by G.I.A. Publications, Inc.,
        from Worship II, Used by permission.

tune: *Cheshire*, adapted by David Hurd, 1978. Adaptation copyright 1978,
        The Church Hymnal Pension Fund. All Rights Reserved.

8 6.8 6.

♩ = 54

Alternate harmonization, H-246a

General Hymns

H-248

Antiphon

Where true love and char-i-ty are found, God him-self is there.

Verses

1 Since the love of Christ has brought us all to-geth-er,
2 There-fore, when we gath-er as one, all to-geth-er,
3 Let us with thy bless-ed ones see thy great beau-ty,

let us then re-joice and be glad to-geth-er,
let us be as one in the Lord, all to-geth-er;
Christ, our God, e-ter-nal-ly en-throned in great splen-dor,

General Hymns

let   ev-'ry-one   fear   and   love   God   all   to-geth-er,
may   care-less thought, ac-tion   or   deed   not di-vide   us;
there   to   pos-sess   joy   with-out   end,   all   to-geth-er,

1 and   let   us   love   one   an-oth-er   with   sin-
2 let   Christ, our   God,   dwell   a-mong   us,   in   ev-

cere   hearts. *(Antiphon)*
'ry   heart. *(Antiphon)*   3 for   in-fi-nite   ag-es

of   ag-es   for   ev-er-more.   A-men.

This is especially suitable for Maundy Thursday.

text: *Ubi caritas et amor, Deus ibi est,* translated by Richard Proulx, 1975.
English translation © 1961-62, World Library Publications, Chicago, IL.
Reprinted with Permission.   12 12.12.12 with refrain

tune: *Ubi caritas,* plainsong melody, Mode vi harmonized by Theodore Marier, 1977.
harmonization, copyright 1978 by The Church Pension Fund.
All Rights Reserved.   ♩ = 60

H-249

1 Ye ser-vants of God, your Mas-ter pro-claim, and pub-lish a-broad his won-der-ful Name; the Name all-vic-to-rious of

2 God rul-eth on high, al-might-y to save; and still He is nigh, his pres-ence we have. the great con-gre-ga-tion his

3 Sal-va-tion to God, who sits on the throne! Let all cry a-loud, and hon-or the Son. the prais-es of Je-sus the

4 Then let us a-dore, and give him his right, all glo-ry and power, all wis-dom and might, and hon-or and bless-ing, with

General Hymns

Je - sus ex - tol;   his King-dom is glo - rious, he rules o - ver all.
tri - umph shall sing,   as - crib-ing sal - va - tion to Je - sus our King.
an - gels pro - claim,   fall down on their fac - es and wor - ship the Lamb.
an - gels a - bove,   and thanks nev-er ceas - ing, and boun - ti - ful love.

text: Charles Wesley, 1744, *alt.*

tune: *New Saraband*, David S. Goodall, 1967. Music Copyright 1967 by David
       S. Goodall, Birkenhead, Merseyside, England. Used by permission
       of the composer.

Alternate tune, H-250

11 11

$\d = 60$

H-250

1 Ye ser-vants of God, your Mas-ter pro-claim,
2 God rul-eth on high, al-might-y to save;
3 Sal-va-tion to God who sits on the throne!
4 Then let us a-dore, and give him his right:

and pub-lish a-broad his won-der-ful Name;
and still he is nigh: his pres-ence we have.
Let all cry a-loud, and hon-or the Son.
all glo-ry and power, all wis-dom and might,

the Name all vic-to-rious of Je-sus ex-tol:
The great con-gre-ga-tion his tri-umph shall sing,
The prais-es of Je-sus the an-gels pro-claim,
and hon-or and bless-ing, with an-gels a-bove,

his king-dom is glo-rious; he rules o-ver all.
as-crib-ing sal-va-tion to Je-sus our King.
fall down on their fac-es, and wor-ship the Lamb.
and thanks nev-er ceas-ing, and in-fi-nite love.

General Hymns

text: Charles Wesley, 1744. *alt.*   11 11

tune: *Paderborn*, melody from the *Catolisch-Paderbornisches Gesang-buch* (1765), harmonized by Sidney Hugo Nicholson. Used by permission of The Proprietors of *Hymns Ancient and Modern*. $o \cdot = 40$

Alternate tune, H-249

Index of Metrical Versions of the Psalms

Index of Metrical Versions of Invitatory Psalms, Canticles and Anthems

Authors, Translators, and Sources

Composers, Sources, and Arrangers

Metrical Index of Tunes

Alphabetical Index of Tunes

Alphabetical Index of First Lines